THE SICILIAN NOBLEMAN'S

Daughter

Blessings –
To Shirley –
Florence Calderone
Blake

THE SICILIAN NOBLEMAN'S

Daughter

A CHRISTIAN TESTIMONY FROM A VIOLENT LIFE

FLORENCE CALDERONE BLAKE

Pleasant Word
A Division of WinePress Group
PW

Pleasant Word (a division of WinePress Publishing, PO Box 428, Enumclaw, WA 98022) functions only as book publisher. As such, the ultimate design, content, editorial accuracy, and views expressed or implied in this work are those of the author.

ISBN 13: 978-1-4141-1496-5
ISBN 10: 1-4141-1496-6
Library of Congress Catalog Card Number: 2009905085

CONTENTS

PREFACE

THE FOLLOWING STORY is true as I have lived and remembered it or as my parents and their siblings relayed it to me. It will reveal secrets that none of my brothers have known before. It also will show some of the amusing eccentricities my family members harbored. To protect their identities, I've changed the spelling of some names in this book. In these cases, I put an asterisk next to that name the first time I mentioned it.

This story contains some violent and shocking moments. I advise against reading it aloud to small children.

May this glimpse into the lives of my zany relatives glorify the perfect God who made us.

—Florence Calderone Blake

Part 1

FROM GIRGENTI TO
CASTELTERMINI, SICILY

Chapter 1

DEFIANT YOUTH

THE NOBLEMAN TOLD me this. His mind seemed lucid when he said it. He related that the first of Mama's ancestors to land in Sicily, Alfonso Navarro, sailed northeast across the Mediterranean from Tunis to Girgenti. Years later, Mussolini would change the seaport's name to Agrigento.

Still independent in 1840, the coveted island hadn't yet been annexed by Garibaldi's Italian forces. The object of frequent invasions over the centuries, Sicily enjoyed an eclectic culture, its own dialect, but no written language. Sicilian speech bore the influence of Portuguese, Spanish, and Italian. Many decades later, words from those languages would still pepper its verbal landscape.

Traditionally, a Sicilian man named his son after that child's grandfather. Because Alfonso, whose given name means "of noble birth," had no sons, his daughter christened her daughter Alfonsa after him.

Although Sicilian society banned dating, marriages weren't strictly family arranged either. A single man became attracted to a nubile woman he'd noticed at church or in the town square. From mutual friends, he'd learn the maiden's identity. Next, he'd request his own father's permission to marry her. With his papa's approval, the suitor would serenade under her balcony, like Romeo and Juliet. He'd then visit her father to ask for her hand in marriage. A future bride didn't speak to a suitor until the wedding day approached, and then only when well chaperoned. Eloping in defiance of parental disapproval meant the unpardonable scandal of dishonoring the family name.

One summer afternoon in 1895, as she drew water at a public well, Alfonsa noticed a handsome eighteen-year-old loitering there. A fading sunlight enhanced the sheen of his raven hair. His suntanned skin seemed an odd contrast to the almost-lilac-blue eyes that studied her.

The young man's innocent yet impish smile engulfed her daydreams. Alfonsa's routine, water-fetching chore would become an unofficial secret rendezvous with him. From giddy girlfriends she learned her admirer's name, Gerlando Scanella.*

"Marriage? You're out of your mind," his father said when Gerlando said he wanted to marry the girl. "What happens to my plans for you to study in Rome and to become a pharmacist like my brother's son?"

"Papa, I love Alfonsa . . ."

"Can she read and write Italian?"

"I don't know."

"Does she have a dowry?"

"I don't care."

"A pharmacist deserves a high-classed, educated woman like a school teacher. I'll find you a nice wife in about eight years."

But each afternoon Gerlando's heart led his feet to the place where he'd first seen Alfonsa. She'd arrive, fill the family's water jug, and then balance it on her head, steadying it with one hand. She'd pretend to look away and depart without a word, but she did communicate through stifled, nervous giggles and eloquent glances.

A month later when Gerlando arrived at the well at 4:00 PM, Alfonsa still wasn't there. Gerlando craned his neck, paced, and wrung his hands. After an hour, determined never to let her out of his sight again, he trudged home. The next afternoon his spirits were revived when she arrived at the well.

"What happened to you yesterday, Alfonsa?" His voice, sounding more nasal than she'd expected, startled her at first.

"I got here late because we had company. Why do you ask? Do you come here just to see me?"

He gave no reply. His tongue suddenly felt swollen and in the way. He studied the cobblestones at his shuffling feet.

"We had relatives visiting," she continued. "My aunt, who's a nun, and the grandfather I'm named after."

"Are you as religious as your aunt?"

She chuckled at the irony of his question. "Auntie and Grandpa wasted many hours trying to convince me to become a nun. Why do you ask?"

"Would it bother you if we didn't have a church wedding? We could get married in a civil ceremony at Casteltermini's municipal courthouse. It would be legally valid."

Now her trembling fingers fumbled with the huge earthen jug on the well's rim. "If you want to marry me, why don't you ask my father?"

"I can't because my father wants to send me away to a pharmacy college in Rome."

Those were stunning words. In most Sicilian cities, pharmacists held the highest prestige. Only the largest metropolises knew the luxury of hospitals or physicians. Elsewhere, the general public revered their local pharmacists and went to them for all medical matters. Gerlando had just admitted he'd put her ahead of honors, wealth, religion, and parental approval.

"Why Casteltermini?"

"I have some relatives there. My cousin's the town's pharmacist, and my aunt and uncle own the general store. Maybe they could help me find housing and work."

"You'd scrap your career plans and elope to Casteltermini rather than receive a sacrament from your church?"

"If you want me, Alfonsa, a carriage will be waiting for you at nine tomorrow morning in the Park of the Doves."

Reason might have shouted to Alfonsa, "Wait. Don't do this. You'll regret it until your dying days." Muted by her heartbeats, such words were wasted on the four-ten, love-struck brunette of fourteen. Would Alfonsa dare to defy a culture that embraced the concept of death before dishonor? Because she lacked the maturity to understand precautions, Alfonsa's decisions would reverberate all the way down to my generation and have powerful effects on my own life.

By traveling together before their civil ceremony and skipping the church rite, Gerlando and Alfonsa scandalized both family names. Brokenhearted relatives disowned them. Unsure of the extent of their parents' wrath, the defiant teens distanced themselves by going to the inland mountain city of Casteltermini. This sits a third of the way between the ports of Palermo to the north and Girgenti (now Agrigento) to the south.

At Casteltermini's pharmacy, Gerlando encountered an icy welcome from his impeccably groomed cousin. "Why don't you make this morally right, Gerlando? Go ask the parish priest to marry you in church."

"We tried to do that right after the civil ceremony. First, the priest wanted our certificates of baptism and confirmation, but we had left them in Girgenti. Then he ranted on about 'disobedience to parents.'"

"Was he wrong? When you have kids, you'll want their unwavering obedience."

Gerlando next called on his aunt and uncle at their general store. Aunt Rosa owned far too much waistline for all the ruffles and gathers that adorned her floral-print skirts. Her gray hair was braided into a bun at the back of her head. Her tar-black eyes topped the bags under them. When she spoke, her surplus chins and sagging jowls bounced like a bulldog's.

Embarrassed by his minor lisp, Uncle Chuzzo seldom uttered more than a few sentences. Snowy haired and emerald eyed, he resembled a railroad engineer in his vertically striped overalls that emphasized his slim frame and skeletal face. While Rosa and Chuzzo wished their nephew success in finding work, they had no job to offer him at their store. The young bridegroom spent the remaining daylight hours canvasing local merchants.

"Around Casteltermini, there are two possible places to find a job," a barber said, "the gristmill or the sulfur mine. Either way you'd work for Don Angelo Calderone. He also owns most of the real estate."

"True," a customer said. "And if you operate a business here, Don Calderone probably owns the lease and collects the rent for it."

As the barber had speculated, Don Angelo Calderone became Gerlando's employer and landlord. The newlyweds moved into a tiny, shabbily furnished flat that they could occupy as a fringe benefit of

Gerlando's job as a sulfur miner. Soon they would be even more cramped for space because their family was about to increase.

The following May, a fifteen-year-old Alfonsa gave birth to her first son, Tommy. Four years later, she became pregnant again.

Early December of 1900 in Girgenti, Gerlando's newly widowed mother, Ninfa, had a premonition. She felt she should step outside and talk to the two young men hitching a donkey-drawn cart to a post. She went out and spied them.

"May I ask where you just arrived from?" she said.

"From Casteltermini, Signora," the men replied.

"There's a family named Scanella living there . . ."

"Professor Scanella, the town pharmacist."

"Do you know his cousin Gerlando?"

"Sure. Gerlando works in the sulfur mine with us. His wife expects her second child soon."

They gave her the address. Ninfa left for Casteltermini immediately. She arrived there on December 8, 1900. Her hired carriage circumvented throngs of people in Casteltermini's annual Feast of the Immaculate Conception parade. When Ninfa reached the house, a local midwife opened the door to the flat where she'd been summoned earlier to deliver Ninfa's new grandchild. When Alfonsa saw her mother-in-law, she cried, laughed, and hugged her.

"If I have a girl, I'm going to name her Ninfa after you," Alfonsa said.

"Please don't send a child through life with that ugly name." Ninfa scanned the procession outside the window. "If it's a girl, name her Maria after Christ's mother."

The jubilant grandmother remained a month after baby Maria's birth. In January Ninfa made a parting vow to her son and Alfonsa. "No matter what the rest of the family says, I promise I'll always be there for you and the children." She kissed them goodbye and returned to Girgenti for the last time. That winter a severe influenza epidemic claimed Ninfa's life.

One cloudy afternoon during the following spring, an urgent pounding on the front door intruded on Alfonsa's lullaby. She admitted a cadaverous-looking, silver-bearded gentleman in faded formal attire, who uttered a word Sicilians dread to hear, *"Coraggio!"* ("Courage!"). It's said to the next of kin of the deceased at wakes and funerals. "I am majordomo for Don Angelo Calderone. He sends his deepest condolences. Your husband, Gerlando, accidentally perished in an explosion at the sulfur mine this morning." He handed her a white rose and a creased envelope, which he'd pulled out of a stack. "I bring you Gerlando's final wages."

Frozen in the daze of denial that follows traumatic news, she couldn't weep. Her voice escalated and cracked in defiance. "He can't be dead. He's only twenty-four years old. Gerlando would have escaped a burning mine . . ."

The ambient silence disagreed. Her shouts dropped to a whimper. "How will I feed my babies?"

"Surely you have relatives who will take you and the children in."

Alfonsa searched her mind and then shook her head.

The majordomo noticed infant Maria in a cradle. "Don Calderone knows your sorrow. He himself lost a spouse to diabetes recently. His baby daughter, Giovanna, needs a wet-nurse."

"Could I earn money doing that until Giovanna is weaned?"

"I'll arrange it for you, Signora."

Sicily's laborers had neither workers' compensation insurance nor government welfare programs. The terms of Gerlando's employment required Alfonsa to vacate the mine employee's quarters. She and her children found temporary shelter in Casteltermini's palace, while she nursed the baby of the wealthiest family in town. Her own daughter developed rickets from the resultant lack of nourishment.

Twenty months passed. Don Angelo Calderone's daughter, Giovanna, was now a toddler. Alfonsa's baby Maria had just turned two. At the close of this workday, Don Calderone's majordomo approached Alfonsa.

"Now that Giovanna has enough teeth, she can be weaned." He proffered an envelope. "Your final wages, Signora. Don Calderone thanks you. Your services in this home are completed."

"Please, could I stay on as a domestic or as a nanny to little Giovanna?"

"No, Don Calderone has enough servants who've been with him for many years. This week he'll remarry. His new wife will rear his children."

The majordomo saw the tears flooding Alfonsa's eyes. "I happen to know of a Sicilian expatriate in the United States who is seeking a Sicilian bride. If you wish, I'll arrange a marriage for you."

"Do you know his name?"

"Salvatore Ventura."

"Salvatore. It means 'one who saves,' doesn't it?"

"And Ventura means 'venture.' Perhaps good omens, Signora."

"Thank you. I'll marry him, but only if he agrees to take both my children to America with us."

Via a cablegram he had dictated to a telegraph office clerk, the non-literate expatriate relayed assurances that he concurred with Alfonsa's terms. He voyaged to Casteltermini for the nuptials and met Alfonsa for the first time. Plump, balding, and graying, Salvatore Ventura looked like Mr. Dithers from the Blondie cartoons. Pixie Alfonsa still seemed more like a preteen Olympic gymnast.

In the vestibule, following a minimal and hastily performed chapel ceremony, Alfonsa gathered her meager belongings for the departure to Palermo's dock. There a ship waited to take them to the United States.

"Tommy, carry this bag. Maria, hold Mama's hand," Alfonsa said.

Ventura grabbed Alfonsa's arm, whisked her to one side, and then dropped the bombshell. "The price of steerage went up. I don't have enough money for four tickets. We only can take you, me, and your boy, Tommy."

"But you assured me that we would be able to take both children."

"And we will, but not right now. I'll save up and buy Maria's ticket in a few months. I promise." He picked up his suitcase. "*The Lombardia* is waiting in Palermo's harbor, ready to sail. We have to leave immediately."

"What'll I do with my little girl?"

"Get someone to look after her for a little while."

Out of alternatives, they hurried to the general store to see Gerlando's aunt and uncle. "I'm so sorry. It's a dire emergency, Aunt Rosa. Could we please leave Maria with you for two or three months? We'll send for her and repay you as soon as possible."

"Alfonsa, you've had two weddings that you never invited us to," Rosa said. "Now you have the nerve to show up here without warning and impose your problems on us?"

"Out of respect for her dead father's memory," Chuzzo said, "we can watch Maria for three months."

Rosa made the sign of the cross, heaved a sigh worthy of Joan of Arc, and kissed the oversized crucifix that hung from her neck. "Very well, three months. May Gerlando's departed soul rest in peace." Then Salvatore Ventura, Alfonsa, and Tommy left Sicily.

Three months passed. A now-pregnant Alfonsa couldn't afford Maria's ticket yet because they'd need the money for doctor bills. Ventura told Alfonsa they would have to keep saving for the ticket "a little while longer." She gave birth to a boy they nicknamed Toto. When Toto reached twenty months of age, Alfonsa delivered another son, Antonio. Fourteen months after Antonio's birth, she gave birth to baby Joe. As each birth drained finances earmarked for Maria's ticket, Alfonsa spent most nights sobbing and calling out her little girl's name.

Chapter 2

WHAT SHE DIDN'T LEARN IN SCHOOL

THE YEARS FLED. Still awaiting the elusive ticket, Rosa and Chuzzo enrolled six-year-old Maria in the first grade. "Now let the teachers have a turn baby sitting her," Rosa said. "I've earned a rest."

At the end of that school day, Maria came home and handed Aunt Rosa a list.

"What does this say? Your Uncle Chuzzo's not here to read it to me."

"The teacher says that I need a pencil, a reader, and a notebook by tomorrow, Aunt Rosa."

"Those cost money. If the school wants you to have them, then the school can supply them, not me."

"But all the kids need them."

"Too bad."

Maria had seen other families come into her aunt and uncle's store to buy similar supplies. She had noted where the merchandise and cash box lay hidden. After the store closed, Rosa usually cooked in the kitchen, and Chuzzo fed the chickens outdoors. The child tiptoed behind the counter and helped herself. From that moment on, she became adept at sneaking, stealing, and hiding whatever necessities Aunt Rosa refused her.

Meanwhile in America, Alfonsa became pregnant for the sixth time, and somehow she had finally scrimped together enough money to buy a steamship ticket to send to Maria.

"Happy ninth birthday, Maria," Uncle Chuzzo said. "Guess what came in today's mail." He handed her an onionskin envelope.

"It's my ticket! Is this real?"

"Yes. You're really getting on the big ship tomorrow."

She kissed and clutched the long-overdue prize to her heart. "Thank you, Uncle Chuzzo. This is the best birthday and the best present anybody could ever want. I'll never forget this one."

"Pack up your clothes," Rosa said.

"You'll have to work in the store without me today," Chuzzo told his wife the next morning. "I'll go hire the carriage for Maria's trip to Palermo."

"Hooray! This is the last time we'll have to spend money on this wretched burden."

"When you get to school, Maria, say good-bye to everyone," Chuzzo said. "At ten o'clock, go to the principal's office and tell him you're withdrawing from fourth grade." Chuzzo checked and wound his silver pocket watch. "I'll come to take you to Palermo where you'll board the ocean liner for New York." He stationed the faded valise stuffed with the child's belongings near the door. "In about two weeks, you'll see the Statue of Liberty, your mother, and all your brothers."

At 10:00 AM Maria fidgeted in the principal's office. She leaped at the sound of every footstep and frowned when she saw it didn't belong to Uncle Chuzzo. Back at the general store, Chuzzo walked in, shook his head, and extended a yellow envelope to Rosa.

"Chuzzo, why are you back so early? Where's the carriage? What's that in your hand?"

"A cablegram from America, Rosa. I just picked it up at the office next to the livery stable. It reads: 'Alfonsa, baby, died in childbirth. Send back ticket. Ventura.'"

"Oh, my God, Chuzzo! What sin did I ever commit to deserve this punishment?"

"The poor kid thought she was having a happy birthday. I canceled the carriage."

"Wait. Go back and reinstate it. Take her to Palermo anyway. Maybe you can find an orphanage there that will take her off our hands. She qualifies now that she's an orphan."

"I don't have the heart—not now at least."

"Pull her out of school anyway. We're too old to be raising and supporting a student."

He arrived at Maria's school an hour late. *"Coraggio,"* he whispered as he patted Maria's chestnut-brown hair, then handed the principal the shocking cablegram.

"She won't be returning to classes. Maria, let's go home. Uncle Chuzzo has some sad news he must give you."

After telling Maria about her mother's death, Aunt Rosa and Uncle Chuzzo explained that they would expect her to pay her way by cleaning the flat and the store. She would run errands. She also would count out the monthly rent payments to landlord Don Calderone's courier. Maria no longer remembered Alfonsa's face, but would often lament, "My mother abandoned me."

In America, Tommy and Maria's stepfather, Ventura, also hired a carriage. He packed his late wife's thirteen-year-old son, Tommy, and his own three sons into it. At sundown, he drove to a rural orphanage run by nuns.

"Toto, Tony, and Joe come with Papa to see the Sisters. Tommy, you stay in the carriage. I'll be right back." He walked his little boys through the wrought-iron archway set in a stone wall and then up a hundred-foot-long graveled pathway. Ventura deposited all three tots on the convent's wraparound porch. "Oops, Papa forgot something. Wait here for a minute. Toto, watch your brothers."

He bolted back to the carriage and drove off. "The nuns said they'd take care of the boys while we get things in order, Tommy. Now, let's go get supper."

"Oh good, Papa! I'm starving. We didn't get to eat breakfast or lunch today."

In an unfamiliar town, Ventura stopped at the first deli he saw. "Go on in, Tommy, and order two sandwiches for us. I'll join you as soon as I tether this horse." Tommy stepped down onto the fragmented, slate sidewalk and then spun around to face his stepfather. "You're not coming back, are you?"

Ventura stared ahead, picked up the leather reins, smacked the horse's rump, and drove out of sight.

The deli owner was tidying the doorstep of his shop in preparation for closing. He hadn't understood the Sicilian conversation, but had seen Tommy burst into uncontrollable sobs. He put down his broom and approached the teen.

"You hungry, kid?"

The boy nodded, but pulled the linings of his pockets inside out to indicate his financial condition.

"Every night the health inspectors make us throw out the food we don't sell. Come on in and help yourself."

Tommy wiped his tears onto a shirt cuff and followed the proprietor into the building. Trays containing remnants of fragrant potato salad, coleslaw, and roast beef slices reinforced the grocer's invitation.

"I usually give it to stray dogs. What's your name, kid?"

"Tommy."

"Well, heck, Tommy, ain't you at least as good as them stray dogs?"

Tommy chuckled, reached for a fork, and dug into the enamel-lined trays as the grocer continued. "Me and my wife live upstairs. There's a cot in the back room down here and an old bicycle. You can sweep floors, make deliveries, eat whatever ain't sold, and sleep on the cot in my storeroom."

Tommy, the Moorish-eyed, five-one tall teenager had only completed the seventh grade, but he had already grown street-smart. For six more years, he remained where he would learn plenty about business, food preparation, and a deli owner's compassionate heart. Tommy told me his story decades later.

A month after abandoning the four boys, Salvatore Ventura booked passage for another round-trip to Sicily. There he acquired his second widowed bride, Miluzza, who also had a son and daughter by her previous marriage. Ventura's face beamed as he held up the one-way ticket that was supposed to have gone to Maria—the ticket for which she had waited seven years. "Here, Miluzza—your wedding gift."

Before World War I, civilian travel between Europe and the United States didn't require passports. Money for passage remained the major obstacle to travel. Since few immigrants had life insurance, Sicilians typically chipped in to help survivors defray funeral costs. For his next surprise, Ventura had skimmed from donations meant for Alfonsa's burial. "I've bought two more one-way tickets, Miluzza, so we can take both your kids with us and raise them together in America."

Ventura would not see his own discarded sons again until they had become embittered grown men.

Chapter 3

FIRST IMPRESSIONS

HER FIRST WORKDAY at Casteltermini's general store brought Maria a new set of problems. She buffed the large glass pane on the entrance door and then overheard shouts in the piazza (town square) outside. A tall, stern-faced man and a shorter, plump man were across the piazza. They waved raised fists at each other. The tall man wore a brown, tweed overcoat with a hem that reached his mid-calf. He pulled a stiletto from his inside pocket.

"Uncle Chuzzo, please come here," Maria said. She peered out again and cringed as the taller man plunged his knife into the other man's chest. The victim collapsed onto the multicolored terrazzo tiles that paved the piazza. His blood drenched the spot.

A yawning Chuzzo entered from the back room, stooped, and hugged the trembling, tongue-tied girl who pointed to the grisly scene.

"Maria, that's Stefano Calderone, Don Angelo's oldest son. His family owns this building, including the part we live in. They have the power to take away our livelihood and our housing." Chuzzo pulled his handkerchief out of his trouser pocket and dabbed Maria's eyes. "If anyone ever asks, say you never saw this man, understand? We call it 'omerta.' The less you see, the better."

She nodded, and Chuzzo returned to his makeshift bunk to continue his afternoon siesta. Moments later, as Maria wiped finger smudges off glass counters, the stabber walked in. "Don Calderone sent me. Where's the rent?"

She reached behind the counter for a white envelope and extended it to Stefano. He counted the contents, rolled his eyes, and sighed. "It's missing ten lire."

"The store owners told me they always pay fifty lire."

"Rents went up to sixty. I mailed notices to everybody. Can't any of these ignorant peasants read?"

From the cash box, she counted another ten lire and set them on the counter. He stuffed them into his pocket, grumbled, and marched out. Within minutes, she heard muffled voices across the piazza, but couldn't discern what was being said. A policeman gripped Stefano's arm, indicated the bloody remains at his feet, and asked heated questions. Stefano shrugged his shoulders and shook his head. Maria tried in vain to hear the conversation that ensued.

"Then how come you have bloodstains on your coat and shoelaces, Calderone?" the policeman said.

"I had a nosebleed," Stefano said.

"And what brings you from your palace down to this neighborhood? Are you slumming?"

"I was collecting rents for my father."

"Any witnesses?"

"Yeah. Ask the little girl in the general store. She saw me, talked to me, and paid their rent about five minutes ago."

The constable ushered Stefano into the store. "Young lady, tell me exactly what you saw this man doing earlier today."

She bit down on her lip at first with Uncle Chuzzo's admonition fresh in her mind.

"Nothing, officer. I never saw him before."

"You lying brat," Stefano said. "You just paid me the rent, remember? It was ten lire short at first."

"Oh, that's right. He came in. I gave him the rent. I didn't know it had gone up, and he got mad. Then I gave him ten more lire."

"Ask your parents to come out here," the constable said.

"My parents are dead, officer."

"Serves you right," Stefano said.

The lawman arrested him. The stabbing never went to trial. Local crime investigators declared the policeman's charges unfounded, and the suspect went free. Maria continued to endure Stefano's sneers whenever he came to collect monthly rents.

When Maria turned fourteen, World War I broke out. Now under the Italian flag, Sicily had allied with the United States. One afternoon, a stout, jovial man in an army private's uniform ducked into the general store. A cloth patch on his pocket bore the embroidered name "Calderone, Gaetano."

"I just want to ditch my pursuer. Mind if I crouch behind your counter?"

Before Maria could answer, a captain came in. "Private Calderone, return to your regiment now, or I'll arrest you for desertion. That carries severe penalties."

"But, I might get killed if I go back."

"You won't get paid if you won't fight for your country."

"I won't get paid if I get killed, either."

Later, the Italian army discharged Don Angelo Calderone's second son, Gaetano, without consequences.

He found creative ways to circumvent another law he considered cumbersome. Before divorce became legal in Italy, he'd tired of his wife, Francesca. He swore out a declaration of insanity and had her confined to a mental institution. He then fled to America with another woman who assumed Francesca's identity. Meantime, the real Francesca languished in an asylum where she died several decades later. In America, the fake Francesca gave birth to another Angelo Calderone, who'd never learn the truth about his parentage. Gaetano would be the only one of the nobleman's siblings I'd ever meet.

On May 10, 1916, in Casteltermini's main piazza (town square), a dark-eyed, charcoal-haired lieutenant captivated Maria's heart with a smile and a wink. She would see him most Sundays near the fountain in the park. One day she watched him buy a fistful of roses from a street vender's pushcart. The lieutenant carried them to the marble bench where Maria sat and presented them to her. A brass name tag on his lapel bore the engraving "Piretti, Emilio." Despite the taboos against speaking to strangers, she reached for the bouquet and sniffed its fragrance.

"Thank you, Lieutenant Piretti."

"Please call me Emilio. I learned your name weeks ago from the old flower peddler. She has told me so much about you."

"Really? What does she say?"

"That your mother left for America without you and didn't return. I will never do this to you, Maria. The day the war ends, I'll outrun cheetahs to get back here to you. Wait for me at this bench."

"I'll be here, Emilio."

"Then we can get married. How many children do you want?"

"Five."

"I like a nice-sized family, too. Five or six."

"Never six. The sixth birth is cursed. That's what killed my mother."

Maria was slim and five feet tall, with shimmering, dark, wavy hair. She had high cheekbones beneath huge, traffic-stopping, hazel eyes. Many young men became instantly infatuated with her. They hoped she would appear on the balcony above the general store to toss them roses. Some of the men hired musicians to serenade her. She ignored them all, remaining loyal to the winsome lieutenant.

November 11, 1918, Armistice Day, was the day that World War I ended. Throngs reveled in Casteltermini's town square. Many spontaneously headed for church. Maria went there first and lit a candle in gratitude to the mother of Jesus—her patron saint and namesake, Maria.

Then she pressed through the crowds to reach the marble bench near the fountain. Amid hordes of revelers, it sat dampened by rain, soiled by confetti and shoe prints, and deserted. For months, she'd return there each day and spend hours alone in anxious vigil.

Rosa and Chuzzo had begun preparations for civil and church ceremonies and a nuptial commemoration. "Maybe today Maria will come back with her Lieutenant Piretti and end our financial drain, Chuzzo."

"I'm uneasy about this, Rosa. Who is this bridegroom? He has never visited our house to ask for Maria's hand. He's never attended our church. What do we know about this man, his family, or his home?"

Rosa frowned. What if Chuzzo was right? She preferred to dismiss the idea.

"I'm sure we'll meet him soon when he returns to Casteltermini."

Lieutenant Emilio Piretti never returned. Maria rationalized his absence by saying he must have died on the battlefield. "Only death would've kept him away." Once again, she tasted the bitterness of abandonment, false hope, and empty promises that further hardened her heart.

On a morning several months later, a man speaking Tuscan, the official dialect of Rome, entered the general store. He identified himself as a detective who had been dispatched to Casteltermini to conduct a missing person's investigation. "Signora Rosa Scanella, do you happen to know a Giovanna Calderone?"

"Why would I know her?"

"As a customer in this store, perhaps? She's your landlord's daughter."

"As far as I know, my landlord's only daughter is Paola. He has a son named Giovanni, but no daughter named Giovanna."

He adjusted his eyeglasses and switched his glance to Maria. "She's about your age, miss. Might you know her from your school years?"

"I'm sorry, officer. I haven't been to school since I was nine. The only Calderone family members I ever remember meeting are the two oldest sons who've been in the store."

"How interesting. A girl from a prominent family lives in a town of several thousand people for eighteen years, yet nobody's ever heard of her."

After the inspector left, Maria told Rosa she vaguely recalled hearing about Giovanna. "Wasn't she the baby my mother wet-nursed years ago?"

"Yes, but Giovanna disgraced the Calderone name. She got pregnant out of wedlock by a married man."

"Where is she now?"

"Her sister, Paola, and brother Giovanni avenged the family honor by mysteriously eliminating her and the baby. Now they deny Giovanna ever existed."

"And we told the detective there was no such person?"

19

"*Omerta,* Maria. Remember, the best word is that which remains unsaid."

How did Rosa know these facts? There had been another witness—an accomplice—I would meet someday.

Chapter 4

DON ANGELO'S CHILDREN

THE WORD *DON* doesn't necessarily mean "Mafia head." It is true that the notorious organized crime families were headed by men respectfully called "Don something or other," but that wasn't the original meaning. The definition of "Don" in this book is "sir" or "mister."

Stereotypical Sicilians have dark hair, brown eyes, and olive complexions. This is a result of the invasion by the Moors and Greeks. But also found among these invaders were the Vikings. Scandinavians in Sicily? Yes, and some fair-skinned, blue-eyed Sicilians descended from them. However, they were so rare that Maria considered them freaks.

Don Angelo Calderone had five sons and two daughters. After his younger daughter Giovanna's murder, no mention of her was permitted among the Calderones.

Like her father and two of her brothers, his other daughter, Paola, had blue eyes, fair skin, and light hair.

By their reputation and from encounters she had had with those who entered the general store, Maria had formed her opinion of the Calderones. They were a race of dogs and brigands. They were nothing but assassins.

The one I call "the Nobleman" had won numerous medals for horsemanship, valor, and expert marksmanship. He'd distinguished himself in battle during World War I. He'd received the title of *Cavaliere*

(Cavalier) from Italy's King Victor Emanuel III. Italian nobility's hierarchy ranked *Cavaliere* as being the lowest and *Principe* (Prince) as being the highest.

Don Angelo's fourth son, Cavaliere Giovanni, lived in their palace attended by servants. He owned horses, elegant clothes, and fine jewelry. Graduation from Europe's comprehensive school curriculum made him literate and well versed in cultural subjects such as opera, literature, and art history. His father had assigned him to manage the sulfur mine.

One Sunday afternoon, the twenty-five-year-old went for a stroll in the piazza, where he spotted Maria feeding pigeons.

"Who's the gorgeous lady in the green dress?" he asked a bystander. "I want to ask her father for her hand."

"She has no parents, Cavaliere Calderone. Maria Scanella is the orphan who was raised by Rosa and Chuzzo of the general store."

Giovanni hurried home to ask for Don Angelo's permission.

"What's wrong with you, Giovanni? An orphan without a dowry? She's socially inferior to us. I can't allow it."

"Father, I beg you, please change your mind. I want her so much."

"Nonsense. We can't risk having a potential gold digger invade our family ranks. Did you know her mother once worked for us as a wet nurse?"

"Oh, now I remember her mother. I was about eight when they left. So that cute little tyke grew up to be that beautiful woman?"

"Enough! You can't marry her. Find someone else."

A few months later, Giovanni suddenly developed a raging fever that didn't respond to medication. Malaria fevers were known occupational risks in Sicilian sulfur mines. In his delirium, he repeatedly called out, "Oh, my Maria. I want my Maria."

Don Angelo made a pact with his son's patron saint and namesake, Giovanni Battista (John the Baptist.) "If my Giovanni survives this illness, I'll permit him to marry his beloved Maria."

Although the Nobleman recovered, the fever had damaged his brain, leaving him with the intellect and explosive temper of a seven-year-old.

With Don Angelo's permission, he visited Maria's uncle Chuzzo to convey the proposal. A fair-skinned, blue-eyed blond, Giovanni stood six feet tall. His high forehead enhanced the length of his nose, disproportionate to his small mouth and chin. Maria preferred swarthy, brown-eyed men like her lost Lieutenant Emilio.

At supper that evening, a gleeful Aunt Rosa raised a wine glass to toast her great-niece. "Don Calderone's son Giovanni has asked to marry you."

"The foreman of the sulfur mine where my father was killed? The people who dismissed my mother from their palace, where, if she'd stayed in Sicily, she would still be alive? Giovanni, the man who murdered his own sister?" Maria's voice escalated. She clenched her teeth and shook her head. "Tell Don Calderone I'd rather be dead than married to a Calderone."

"We can't always have what we want, Maria."

"But he's the ugliest one of that disgusting lot. Please, Aunt Rosa, anybody on earth, but not him."

"You don't say no to Don Angelo Calderone's son. We've accepted the proposal. The civil and church ceremonies are set for January ninth, three days before your twentieth birthday."

Maria never spoke about the ceremonies, civil or religious, or of the early days in this marriage to which she felt involuntarily enslaved. Neither she nor the Nobleman nor any of his relatives told me anything about his grandparents. Perhaps they died young, and Giovanni never knew them. Whatever the reason, that branch of the family tree remained mysterious.

In October of 1921, Maria bore a son, upon whom Giovanni dutifully conferred Don Angelo's name. Sicilian traditional systems are confusing and amusing when brothers all name their sons after their grandpa. In this case, it resulted in six Angelo Calderones. For clarity, they'd be called Angelo Calderone of whichever son had sired them. On legal documents, Giovanni's first boy was Angelo Calderone di Giovanni. Unaware of these technicalities, Ellis Island workers sometimes erroneously issued papers attributing these appendixes as surnames to Sicilians immigrating to the United States.

Early in 1923, the family patriarch, Don Angelo, summoned his sons to a meeting. Gaetano, the one who had fled Sicily after fraudulently institutionalizing his wife for being insane, was the only one missing.

"Fascism under Benito Mussolini gains power that can devastate our family's income," Don Angelo said. "The Fascists seek to take over all industry. If they succeed, we lose everything—the sulfur mine, gristmill, stores, and apartment buildings." He moved his chair closer and lowered his voice. "But Mussolini's enemies, 'The Black Hand Society' or 'the Mafia,' have arrived in Casteltermini. They destroy their opponents and claim responsibility by leaving a black glove or handprint at the scene. Which group should we ally with, the Fascists or the Mafia?"

Stefano, the oldest, spoke first. "Papa, we can't lose to the Fascists and hand over Casteltermini to them. I'd join any group that would help me fight them."

Each of the others in turn agreed that if they had to pick sides, they'd rather choose the anti-Fascists—the Mafia.

"Mussolini plans to speak at our amphitheater Monday at 10:00 AM," Don Angelo said.

"Papa, we're forgetting something," Stefano said. "At this table sits one of the best sharpshooters in Sicily. Hand Giovanni a rifle and turn him loose on 'il Duce.'"

"I'd gladly be the sniper to eliminate Mussolini," Giovanni said.

Don Angelo folded his arms and leaned back to weigh this unanticipated option. Giovanni would need to score a bull's-eye on the first shot. Had he retained his memory, physical strength, and acute vision? With the crowds that were anticipated, a near miss could spell chaos. Did this brain-damaged former artilleryman still have his marksmanship skills?

The eldest brother took the younger brother to their secluded villa's spacious lawn for intense target practice. Two hours later, a confident Stefano reassured the Don. "Papa, your Cavaliere Giovanni could probably shoot the wings off a mosquito in midflight from ten kilometers away."

Monday morning, Giovanni stretched in a prone position, using his elbows for support, behind wild shrubs on a hillside. With loaded rifle cocked and trained on the amphitheater's speaker's platform, he eyed his intended target, the man at the podium. Then the marksman's rapid heartbeats decelerated. It was not Mussolini's bald head and babyish face that he saw. The dictator, aware that he had too many foes in Casteltermini, had sent an assistant in his place. A dozen uniformed, armed guards flanked the substitute orator on both sides.

Now convinced that Fascism would outlast the Mafia, Giovanni vowed, "Rather than serve Mussolini, I will take my family to America."

Because of strict immigration quotas and rules, however, getting to the United States would prove grueling. He'd need to obtain American citizenship, which required his studying the language and passing written tests in English. Italy's Fascists ordered him to relinquish all rights to any family wealth and to leave with only the barest essentials.

His tenure in the sulfur mine had helped Giovanni develop a tolerance for abnormally high temperatures. That would serve him well a little later on. Meanwhile, alone in America, he labored, studied, and saved. Seven years passed before his wife and son saw him again. A lot had happened during those seven years.

Chapter 5

A MYSTERIOUS BIRTH
AND DEATH

DURING GIOVANNI'S PROLONGED absence, Maria gave birth to her second son in Sicily. She named him Gerlando after the father she'd lost in her infancy. Four different relatives gave me conflicting accounts of this child's date of birth. According to the Nobleman, Maria told him she had the baby eight months after her Giovanni's departure for America. Maria's oldest son, Angelo (Ang), insisted this brother was born twelve months after his father left Sicily. Maria related varying dates and stories to my sister, Lee, and me.

Why not just check the date on the birth certificate? Even if a written birth record were found, that wouldn't clarify the birth date. Italian law required midwives to register births by taking newborns to Municipal Hall in person. This was to prevent falsifying any child's gender, thereby evading future military obligations. The midwife usually had to walk to town carrying the infant. Because of weather or time constraints, they often delayed these registration errands for weeks or months. Ang would say, "I was born on October 21, but was registered on October 28."

Although Maria often recounted her grandmother Ninfa's story of naming her on Mary's feast day, December 8, Maria's birth records read "January 12, 1901." For a price corrupt midwives could be convinced to "forget" the registration process entirely.

But back to the birth of Gerlando. Ang said he'd occasionally come home from school to find a male visitor present. The man would seem startled by the boy's arrival and would rush out of the flat. When he asked who the man was, Maria replied, "Just someone who likes us. Don't ever tell anyone about him."

The date of the baby's death is as mysterious as that of his birth. Maria told my sister, Lee, that baby Gerlando was born January 12, 1923, and died February 24, 1924, at age thirteen months. If Pop left Sicily after Ang had turned two, as Ang, Maria, and Pop confirmed, the historical details don't jibe. Ang's second birthday fell on October 21, 1923. Mussolini became Italy's prime minister that year. As of January, Pop hadn't yet departed for the United States.

"Giovanni's sister Paola entered our flat in Casteltermini one day while I nursed Gerlando," Maria said. "Paola started shouting accusations and calling me vile names. A 'bolt of emotional shock' poisoned my milk and instantly killed my six-month-old on the spot." When someone asked Maria what Paola might have been accusing her of that was so upsetting, she said she couldn't remember.

On one occasion, Maria said, "The baby shriveled and became paralyzed from the 'bolt of bad milk' and died a few weeks later." I often wondered, if Maria truly believed emotional trauma could poison milk, why would she later nurse her next three babies? She had also said, "If Gerlando's constant crying riled me enough, I'd pick him up by one arm and fling him against the wall. That would shut him up."

Decades later, the Nobleman told me he had sent Maria money to pay for the baby's eighteen-month hospital stay in Palermo. Did the first Gerlando Calderone die at age six months, as Maria had told me? Did he die at thirteen months, as she'd reported to Lee, or was it the eighteen months she'd recounted to the child's absent father? So far, numerous computer searches have failed to turn up any record of the child's birth or death. Apparently, neither was ever recorded. Nobody now on earth knows what illness or injury ended the little one's life or at what age.

A MYSTERIOUS BIRTH AND DEATH

Late in December of 1930, Giovanni returned to Sicily with tickets for himself, Maria, and nine-year-old Ang. He found the boy in the khaki uniform worn in Fascist-controlled schools where Ang had learned songs such as "*Giovinezza*" (youth), which praised Fascism. Among the textbooks the school mandated was one Mussolini had authored titled *God Does Not Exist*. Giovanni yelled, stomped, tore the uniform off the boy, banned him from singing Fascist songs, and burned the offensive book.

Soon, with just their traveling clothes, the three boarded the SS *Augustus*. To avoid paying an additional fare, they kept secret another of Maria's pregnancies. Eleven days later, Maria's heart leaped at the view from the liner's deck. "See that, Angelo? At last, there's the statue with the raised torch, greeting our arrival in New York Harbor. I've waited almost thirty years for this moment." However, while she learned that the doors to America swung open, she soon learned how the doors to housing or jobs slammed shut on "ignorant greenhorns who could hardly speak the language."

They first located the Nobleman's only brother living in the United States. Gaetano, with his common-law wife and their son, Angelo Calderone di Gaetano, occupied a flat in Paterson, New Jersey. They had chosen "The Silk City" located about fifteen miles northwest of Manhattan because its numerous textile mills sometimes hired unskilled laborers.

Someday I would meet my extroverted uncle Gaetano and his entertaining son, also named after Don Angelo. Gaetano would recount true stories that most of our family had never heard before about the Nobleman's horsemanship, marksmanship, and military accomplishments.

The first advice Gaetano offered his younger brother was "Americanize your names. Giovanni in English is 'John,' and Maria is 'Mary.' Next, take any job and any housing you can find. Forget the respectful bows, the palace, and the terrazzo floors. They're gone. There are no gold-paved streets in America."

Here's where John made use of his extraordinary tolerance for heat. "The Dye House needs somebody to tend conveyer belts in the fabrics' drying rooms," Gaetano continued. "These departments exceed

29

a hundred degrees even in winter with the outside doors wide open. The pay is miserable, and few people can do this job without getting heatstroke."

"I'll do it," John said. "Remember what we'd say in Sicily. 'When better is missing, worse improves.'"

Nobody but slumlords would rent to them. Only recent immigrants or oppressed minorities would settle for their vermin-infested flats in the seediest, most crime-ridden parts of town.

Several months after their arrival in America, Maria gave birth to a daughter she adored. Following tradition, the baby should be named Carmella, after John's mother.

"Let's name her Lina," Maria suggested, "and say it's short for Carmelina."

A year following Lina's (Lee's) birth, Maria had a boy, Gerlando II (Jerry). Two years later, Maria had another boy and named him Emilio (Mil). John wanted to call him Victor Emanuel, in loyalty to the monarch, but Maria insisted on "Emilio" and never explained why.

The furniture in their run-down flat was comprised of an eclectic combination of Salvation Army rejects that truly supported the phrase "When better is missing, worse improves." The squalor of the slums prompted Maria to seek employment so that she could save enough money to own a home one day.

World War II brewed in Europe and threatened to erupt there. A growing manpower shortage enabled her to find a job making men's coats in a sweatshop. She sewed collars and cuffs by hand and was paid by the piece. Soon after she'd begun work and arranged for the children's daycare, an unplanned setback torpedoed her hopes. She'd once again become pregnant.

"I can't go through this cursed sixth pregnancy, John. I know it'll kill me to have another baby. Find a way, legal or not, to get rid of it."

He dismissed her pleas with "If it's a boy, this time we'll name him Victor Emanuel. If it's a girl, she'll be Alfonsa after your mother."

She pretended to accept the inevitable. "No. I don't even want to hear the name of that wretched monster who abandoned me. If it's a girl, we'll call her Florence."

A MYSTERIOUS BIRTH AND DEATH

A few months later, a distant cousin wrote from Agrigento. She'd had a daughter and named her Alfonsa to honor Maria's mother. Now the Sicilian obligation to save face and receive peer approval kicked in.

Late in 1935, Maria gave birth to me. "John, we'll have to put the name Alfonsa on the birth and baptismal certificates. Otherwise, people will think we're terrible." Although they officially gave me her mother's name, she would rarely use it. She would refer to me as Florence and only address me as Alfonsa in expressions of anger or scorn.

Part 2

EARLY YEARS OF
A PATERSON SLUM KID

Chapter 6

THE TARGET CHILD

She treats her young harshly, as if they were not hers.
—Job 39:16 (NIV)

I FIRST HEARD the term "target child" when I took courses in child abuse issues at Cornell as education for my job in child protective services. "Some parents," the professor explained, "select one child as the target of their contempt." Factors that bring this about may be any of the following:

- The child has a name the parent dislikes.
- The child is named after someone the parent hated.
- The child resembles someone the parent detests.
- The pregnancy was unwanted or the delivery painful.
- The birth occurred at an inopportune time.

Guilty on all counts, I was the only one of Mom's children who resembled Papa's side of the family. Pop's brother, Gaetano, called me the image of his sister, Paola. During some of Mom's tirades, she addressed me as "Aunt Paola." Mom labeled me as one of "that race of dogs and assassins."

When she brought me home from the hospital, my siblings had the highly communicable childhood disease whooping cough. Had the hospital staff known this, they would have placed the house under quarantine, and I would not have been allowed in it. But as it was, I contracted the disease and struggled to breathe. A neighbor alerted the board of health. They returned me to the hospital and saved my life.

"That obnoxious, meddling man downstairs," Mom said. "Why couldn't he stay out of it and just let her die?"

When I was three weeks old, Mom enrolled us in a day nursery run by the charity then called the "Community Chest." Mom returned to her factory job. Fourteen-year-old Ang pushed the baby carriage and walked four younger siblings to and from the nursery before and after his classes.

The nursery staff spoke English. At home we spoke Sicilian. Unlike our older siblings, who couldn't understand English when they started school, Mil and I were bilingual from the start. The two women in charge of the nursery were devout Christians. God put them in our lives, where he used them for his loving purposes.

Mom was steadily employed for ten months. She commuted to and from work by bus, and she ignored the increasingly sharp intestinal pains she felt. By my first birthday, a burst appendix forced her into a hospital bed. "We'll do our best," the doctor told Pop, "but your wife probably won't live."

One day my dad took a page from Ventura's book of fatherhood. Pop came home, packed us all up, and attempted to enroll us in a nearby Catholic orphanage. "We can't accept these children," the nun said. "They're not orphans. Even if, God forbid, your wife should die, they'd still have one parent."

Pop brought us back to our unheated second-story flat. "I'm going away long enough for all you kids to starve or freeze to death. Then, when I get back, I'll have five less problems to worry about."

"No more milk deliveries," he told our milkman. "I can't afford it."

God had that covered. "Pay me when you have it, Mr. Calderone," the dairy owner—also a Christian—replied. "Your babies need milk to stay alive."

As for the older children's food, God had covered that detail too. Remember Alfonsa's three sons by Salvatore Ventura? Mom's now grown half brothers chipped in and brought a huge basket of assorted fruit interspersed with mixed nuts to her hospital ward. Mom's condition precluded solid food. Now fifteen, Ang was the only child permitted to visit Mom. "Take that fruit basket home," she said. "It will just go to waste here."

God used the basket of fruit to sustain us over the next eighteen days. For heat, Ang gathered coal that tumbled off the Erie Railroad freight cars onto the tracks near our flat. He burned the fuel in our kitchen wood/coal stove.

By another of God's gracious acts, while Mom fought for life in her hospital bed, a stranger walked in and handed her a thick, black book. On the cover in gold letters was the title in Italian, "La Sacra Bibia" (The Holy Bible). He may have been a member of the Gideon's or the New York Bible Society. He could have been sent by the women who ran the day nursery, who knew Mom was there and that she couldn't read English. "The Lord gave the word: great was the company of those that published it" (Ps. 68:11 KJV).

That Thanksgiving Day, Mom remained confined, and Pop continued absenting himself. We had not a morsel of solid food left in the house, and if there had been food, there would have been nobody capable of cooking it. At noon, someone knocked on the back door and then left before Ang could open it. The blended aromas of a classic American Thanksgiving banquet greeted our nostrils. On the stair landing sat a corrugated cardboard box containing a warm, fully cooked turkey with all the trimmings. None of us had ever tasted turkey meat, gravy, stuffing, or cranberry sauce before. That bounty and its remnants kept us alive until Mom's improved condition restored Pop's confidence and he returned home.

The day nursery staff had placed our names on their church elders' list of needy families in the community. Because I was still a baby, I don't recall these events. When I hear them retold, I marvel at the loving God who provides directly and through his believers.

The year my brother Mil turned four, he became eligible for a pre-kindergarten near the parochial school our siblings Lee and Jerry attended. Because it was more convenient to send me there too, Mom "added" six months to my age. "If anybody asks how old you are, say, 'I'm four,' and hold up four fingers. If they ask your birthday, say, 'May 6.'" That would have made Mil eight months older than I was. Otherwise, either we were twins or one of us was premature. For years I thought I had two birthdays.

Newcomers to a country tend to cluster with others from the same town of origin. It lessens the culture shock. To our delight, we had some *paisani* (fellow countrymen) in Paterson. The tendency to group together didn't help their mastery of English though. Our parents would patronize Italian-speaking barbers and venders. They'd work with Italians and speak only Italian dialects to acquaintances or relatives. Decades later, they still couldn't speak English without a strong Italian accent. Mom refused any help with her English. She insisted, "Americans understand what I mean. It doesn't matter if it isn't said perfectly."

Mom and Pop became close friends with a couple named Joe and Grace Lobo,* also from Casteltermini. When they had a daughter, Millie, they asked my mother to be the child's godmother in baptism. This made Mom Grace's *comare* (co-mother), sealing a special spiritual bond. We children were to use the honorific *comare* when addressing Grace, and her offspring would address our mom the same way.

Baby Millie and I formed a close friendship. Our mothers entered a covenant: "When Florence turns twelve or so, Grace will sponsor her confirmation at church." That double sealed the "co-mother" pact between them. Many Americans I've met misunderstood this true definition of the words *comare* and *compare* (co-father). They thought it meant "comrade."

I enjoyed our frequent visits to the Lobo's second story flat located just four blocks from ours. Few of us had telephones or cars, and nobody expected any warning when we planned to drop in. Around twilight one summer evening, we arrived to find the Lobos had a new neighbor downstairs. She was an obese woman with snowy hair, and she rested on a backless garden bench that sagged under her weight. At first, she blinked. Then a smile creased her face, and she greeted Mom in Sicilian. Her voice, hoarse and gravelly, sounded almost masculine.

"Maria, don't you remember me? I'm Annina, the midwife from Casteltermini."

"You live here now?"

Annina nodded. "Who's the cute little girl with you? Is this the baby you were having when…?"

"She's my youngest. Well, I've got to rush home to start supper."

We'd already eaten supper. "Mom, aren't we going to visit the Lobo family upstairs?" I asked.

"Not now; we have to go."

When I asked Mom later why this woman had her so agitated that we couldn't go to see our friends, she said that was a secret.

The following day Mom announced, "We don't talk to Joe and Grace Lobo anymore. They betrayed our friendship." Mom's official explanation was that when she'd tried to buy furniture on credit, the store manager asked, "Do you have any credit references?"

"What does that mean?" Mom asked.

"Someone who can vouch for your ability to pay your bills."

"Joe and Grace Lobo know us. They recently bought furniture from you," Mom said she told the store owner.

My parents' credit history included an eviction for missing rent payments when I was born. Also, unlike Joe and Grace, Mom and Pop had no proven track record of a major credit purchase yet. Within days, a letter from the furniture retailer arrived denying their application.

After that day, Mom character-assassinated the Lobos to us and to our other *paisani*. "The Lobos blocked us from getting nice new furniture," she said. "They said we're bad payers."

Without ever asking the Lobos whether the retailer had contacted them or what they'd replied, Mom simply cut them off. She would nurse this grudge for more than a decade.

Chapter 7

MY ALLIANCE WITH THE NOBLEMAN

ANYTIME MOM AND Pop were both at home, we could expect shouts, curses, and flying objects within twenty minutes. I am not exaggerating. The only exception was when we had company. Then they behaved like saints. If Mom wanted to buy something and Pop didn't agree, she'd keep fighting until she got what she wanted. Often she'd continue provoking him, even though I'd see him slap or punch her. If we kids tried to protect her from his fists, she'd scream at us to stay out of it.

Many Saturdays when we were all home, she'd tell Pop, "Get out of my sight. I can't stand to look at you another minute." Then she'd glare at me and say, "And take that one with you."

Yes, he was violent, cruel, and probably guilty of murder. Yet around me, Pop was the perfect, respectful gentleman. We were both outcasts in Mom's eyes, both resembling "that race of dogs." He and I were part of his circle—not hers. Pop would take me on errands and to museums, libraries, galleries, and cathedrals. Sometimes having me along helped him through his language barrier. His noble bearing became evident in the way he'd tip his hat to a lady or remove it in an elevator. He imparted to me his love of fine architecture, music, and art. If I learned any modicum of manners, it was largely due to this Nobleman's example.

The difference between going somewhere with Mom or with Pop was this: Mom would say, "We found the county building. Hurry up.

Ask that lady where room 205 is. There's a man with a wristwatch. Ask him what time it is. Here's the elevator. Quick, let's go."

But Pop would say, "This is the county building, Florence. These steps are made of pure granite. Look at the mosaic pattern on the floor in the foyer. Now look up at the ceiling in the rotunda. See how the light makes a prism with all those rainbow colors."

We'd stroll through the lobby to another area. "That mural depicts Alexander Hamilton signing documents while founding Paterson. He named it after William Paterson, the governor of New Jersey at the time." My siblings viewed this alliance with Pop as favoritism, and they resented me for it.

As the start of elementary school approached, I was only four. Pop took me to a low-cost clinic at the board of health for my immunizations. We sat and waited for the doctor and chatted softly in Sicilian, discussing Papa's favorite subject—grand opera. When the physician arrived, a desk clerk, unaware that we understood English, said that another uncultured, dumb ginzo kid was there for immunizations. The clerk motioned for us to go in.

To distract me from the needles' stings, the doctor kept me in conversation. He began by asking me what school I'd be entering.

"Saint Anthony's, doctor."

"You'll learn a lot of new things there, like the Lord's Prayer. Do you know what the Lord's Prayer is?"

"Sure. At church we sing it in Latin, and at home we recite it in Italian, but in nursery school we say it in English."

"Do you have any questions for me?"

"Yes. What does 'uncultured' mean?"

He blushed. "It means, well, some people don't know some things about art and music."

"We know some things about art and music."

"Oh yeah? What's your favorite song?"

"The 'Toreador Song' from *Carmen*."

"Carmen? Is that an Italian opera?"

"No. The story happens in Seville, Spain, but they usually sing it in French because Georges Bizet composed it in French."

"Who wrote Romeo and Juliet?"

"Do you mean the play or the opera?"

A nurse entered the room. "Doctor Green, is Romeo and Juliet also an opera?"

"Don't ask me, ask the 'uncultured' kid here," Doctor Green said.

"Yes, the play in English was what William Shakespeare wrote," I said, "but there's also an Italian opera called '*Giulietta e Romeo*.'"

Pop joined the conversation. Here was a game he delighted to play with me at home or among his friends. "Florence, tell them who composed Madam Butterfly."

"Giacomo Puccini."

"What else did he write?"

I had memorized that by rote. "*Tosca* and *La Boheme*."

I didn't understand why the physician grinned. I thought everyone knew these things.

"You mentioned art," the doctor said. "I'll bet you can't tell me who painted the *Pieta*?"

I giggled. "Oh, that's a trick question. The *Pieta* is not a painting; it's a sculpture by Michelangelo Buonarotti."

He injected my arm and watched me wince. He continued quizzing me on several other composers and art masters; I kept furnishing the answers.

"Young lady, how did you learn these things?"

"My father told me."

After he completed my immunizations, the physician walked out to the desk clerk.

"Hey Marge, does your kid know who sculpted the *Pieta* or who composed *Carmen*, *Tosca*, or *La Boheme*?"

"Of course not, he's only fifteen."

"Call them 'poor' or 'disadvantaged.' But don't ever call these two people 'uncultured, dumb ginzos' around me again," he said.

Despite his shortcomings, Papa taught me to love and respect my culture and heritage. He also taught me to honor the American flag and "the land of the free." The only thing he taught me to hate was dictatorship.

By then, I had a genuine Sicilian godfather, but not the kind you see in the movies. Sicilians took the godparent role quite seriously. Equating a godparent with Saint John, who baptized Jesus, my relatives would never speak ill of one, without first uttering the disclaimer, "preserving Saint John."

When I was an infant, "So relatives would approve," Mom said, she wanted me to be baptized into the church she'd stopped attending. For the godparent, she chose her half brother, Toto. The oldest of the tots Salvatore Ventura had once abandoned, Toto now rented a room in the tenement his father and stepmother, Miluzza, owned. It was located two blocks from our flat.

Toto was to function as my spiritual advisor in the event of my own parents' incapacity. Like all of Mom's brothers, he had inherited short, dark, and hair-deprived genes. If you picture the Quaker Oats logo (except sporting a fringe of black strands around a bald pate), you're picturing Toto.

I was four and a half the summer my oldest brother, Ang, left home to join the Marine Corps. To save one dollar per week in childcare costs, Mom withdrew her four youngest from daycare and put nine-year-old, Lee, in charge of them at home when Pop worked day shifts.

"Since I work steady nights and live nearby, I'll check on your kids' safety during the days," Toto said.

"How nice of you," Mom told him.

"It's no trouble, Maria."

Toto came by frequently with his camera. He snapped many pictures of us girls, but none of my brothers. One he took of me in my summer hand-me-down rags shows a soot-laden wall of our run-down housing unit. He had copies of that photo enlarged.

Toto grew friendly with Dottie, a child who lived downstairs from us. He'd dispatch my brothers to the movies with a quarter and hang around our flat. His conversation became bolder. He'd tell my sister, Lee, his plans regarding Dottie.

She wasn't home one day when he planned to visit her. He gave my brothers coins to go see Roy Rogers fighting bad men and riding a white palomino that never got dirty. Annoyed by Dottie's absence, Toto followed Lee into our parents' bedroom. I stood in the room facing Pop's dresser, my tiny fingers playing tag with the gold sweep-second hand on the alarm clock's crystal. With my back to them, I couldn't hear their whispered conversation.

Toto asked Lee a completely improper question. She emphatically declined. Suddenly, his face red with rage, he lunged at me, grabbed my shoulders, and whisked me into the adjacent bedroom. He slammed me down on my back so hard I bounced on the bed twice. I interpreted his actions as punishment for touching Pop's alarm clock.

What transpired in the next ninety seconds was a brutal violation. Wild-eyed fury replaced the usually mellow smile on Toto's face. I remember severe pain, pressure, and intense fear. At one point, he pulled back briefly and then started toward me again. Now abandoning "respect for my elders," I kicked wildly with both feet. My oft-repaired, thickly resoled shoes like heavy clogs landed solidly in his groin area. The look of overpowering rage turned into a painful wince. Toto backed away and hobbled out of the house.

My sister had watched him grab me and disappear into the next room. "What happened?" she asked.

"I don't know, Lee. He was hurting me, and his extra finger was out."

Shortly afterwards, Toto returned. "Lee, don't tell anybody about this. If anyone finds out, I could go to jail."

As soon as Mom arrived home from work, Lee told her everything.

"Don't ever let your father know," Mom said. "If he does, he'll kill Toto to avenge the family honor. Then Pop will go to the electric chair, and we can't manage without his income."

She pointed at me. "So now I bear the stigma—she's no longer a virgin. How will I ever find a husband for her? She can never marry a nice man; good men want their brides to be virgins."

I had no idea what she meant, but I knew that whatever had happened was worse than I'd imagined. It could mean jail for Toto, and Pop would kill him over it. The attack left me with a terror and mistrust of most males and with feelings of being inferior "damaged goods."

After that day, Toto avoided visiting when our parents weren't home. Months later, my sister stumbled upon pornographic material he'd hidden in our storage closet. Also stored there was a copy of the photo he'd taken of me and enlarged. Pop and my brothers never knew about this man's perversion or the lasting harm he'd done to me.

The following December, Toto came to the house on a Saturday and asked to speak to Mom. I saw him remove a beige business-sized envelope from his overcoat's inner pocket and hand it to her. He also gave Mom Christmas gifts for Lee and for me, but nothing for my brothers. Before then, no one, not even our parents, had ever given us Christmas presents. Lee's was a set of bath salts. Mine, a pretentious gold bracelet with a heart bangle attached, seemed inappropriate for a messy, raggedly dressed child my age. Mom forbade me to wear it or even take it out of its original gift box. I started hating the name of Dorothy's dog, Toto, in *The Wizard of Oz* because it was the same name as his.

The gifts, usually consisting of women's jewelry, came every Christmas. One year he dropped by with a young female relative, handed Mom a box for me, but nothing for my siblings.

"Why is your dress torn?" Mom asked the girl, who then glared at Toto.

"Don't ask me, ask him."

As usual, the beautiful necklace and matching, long dangly earrings he'd brought were age-inappropriate. Mom again forbade me to wear them, and he'd again wasted his money.

Jerry and Mil envied the preferential treatment Toto showed me. To justify it, Toto would say that a godchild is somewhat special. My brothers remained oblivious to the guilty conscience that motivated Toto's gifts. This man's vicious attack and Mom's reaction to it would scar my life and personality thereafter.

Toto snapped this backyard photo of Florence, age four, and had it enlarged.
The house, actually white, looked mostly blackened by soot
from nearby factory smokestacks.

Chapter 8

THE NOBLEMAN'S TEMPER IN PUBLIC

THE NAME OF the group misled him. In Sicily, Pop had belonged to a political party called "The Christian Democrats." He learned from local sources that an organization calling itself "The Italian Democratic Club" was forming in Paterson. The founders, who hailed from Italy's mainland, invited Pop to join. He took me to its first meeting held in a storefront with bare wooden floors. A potbelly stove dominated the center of the room. The lack of furniture and window coverings caused voices and the stove's crackling wood to echo. The group's president spotted me. "John, you brought your little granddaughter."

This was a common mistake. Forty-one when I was born, Pop knew his prematurely gray hair added years to his appearance.

"I'm not his granddaughter. I'm his daughter."

The now red-faced man swept his gaffe aside with "What do you want to be when you grow up, honey?"

"A school teacher."

"Good for you. Teachers are really respected in Italy."

"That's what my mother always says. That's why I want to be one, so she'll be proud of me and like me."

"We're starting our meeting now, so you sit and watch us and learn, okay?"

I observed from the sidelines. The group sat in a semicircle of folding chairs. They stood up when their leader set a 12-by-16-inch portrait on an easel. It was of Benito Mussolini. The men took turns saluting it and shouting, *"Viva il Duce!"* ("Long live the captain!").

Pop lunged forward, seized the portrait, and smashed it repeatedly against the cast iron stove, breaking the glass into shards. Then he ripped out the picture and flung it into the stove's roaring flames.

"John, calm down," the chairman said. "You'll scare the kid."

Having witnessed Pop's violent temper outbursts almost daily, I'd grown used to his behavior. This time I considered it heroic. Pop never returned to that club again, and it soon disbanded.

Two months before my fifth birthday, I started primary school at Saint Anthony's, the parochial school three of my older siblings attended. Primary was kindergarten without the fun. A rat-infested major fire hazard, the building had long been condemned by the health department yet remained in use. The understaffed city government hesitated to impose fines against a church.

In those days, parochial schools and Roman Catholicism were nothing like today's post-ecumenical versions. Run by strict old-world Italian nuns, our school and church operated more like monarchies than faith systems. At church, except for a brief sermon either in English or Italian, Mass was hurriedly mumbled and occasionally sung in Latin. Usually nobody there besides the priest understood the words.

The church precepts mandated that we attend Mass on Sundays and on "holy days of obligation." The latter included January 1, celebrated as the feast of Christ's circumcision under Jewish custom. Except for severe illness, failure to comply with church precepts was deemed a mortal sin, punishable by eternal fire. However, Mom, who expected us to attend Mass daily, absented herself from regular church services. The mixed message confused me.

Among our religion's many rules, we gleaned some information I valued. We were taught an encapsulated version of the Ten Commandments, some parables, the beatitudes, and selected Bible stories. However, we were forbidden to read a book about religion unless it bore an imprimatur of the pope or his cardinal. This ruled out any versions of the Bible then available to the general public.

One morning that fall, new pictures graced Saint Anthony School's corridor. Amid the usual array of cardinals and saints, there now hung portraits of Italy's king and queen. Between these two, someone had added a 30- by 24-inch portrait of Benito Mussolini in a military captain uniform. Its brushed, antique-gold, ornate frame made it conspicuous in its place of honor.

"Mussolini is a bad man. He wrote a book called *God Does Not Exist*," my sister told Mother Superior. "My brother Ang had to read this textbook at school in Sicily."

"How dare you say that?" the nun said. "Mussolini's a great man. He has brought Italy progress—good roads and obligatory schooling."

That Sunday evening, Lee told Pop, "There's a big picture of Mussolini in the hall at school."

"Not for long," Pop said. "I'm on the afternoon shift this week, so I'm home in the mornings."

Monday from my classroom, I heard violent smashing and shattering of glass coming from the corridor. Voices rose to shouts. Mother Superior sent the school's janitor to find the local traffic cop.

When Officer Murphy arrived, she told him Pop had smashed the expensive frame, taken its contents outside, and burned it.

"What was in the frame, sister?"

The nun hesitated and looked at the janitor.

"A portrait of the pope," the custodian said. "I hung it myself."

Mother Superior stood by, neither confirming nor denying it.

Papa's rage worsened his thick accent. The only word Officer Murphy could decipher was "Mussolini."

"Please take this man into your office, Mother Superior. Does he have a child in school who can interpret for me?"

The nun could have summoned any one of my older siblings. But she sent the school's pet nerd to fetch me, the youngest, and she thought the least likely to know a Fascist dictator from a pontiff.

"Do you walk through these halls every day, little girl?" Murphy asked.

"Yes, officer."

"Whose pictures are over this door?"

"The man is King Victor Emanuel III of Italy, and the lady is the queen."

"Was there a picture of the pope between these two this morning?"

"No, the pope is that man in the white, shiny clothes on the other wall. The picture that was here before was of Benito Mussolini."

"Who's Benito Mussolini?"

"A bad man in Italy."

"What does he look like?"

"He has no hair, a fat face, a brown jacket with ribbons on it, and a hat that looks like a boat."

Murphy asked the nun to bring my father back. He gripped Pop's hand, patted his back, and said, "Thanks, mister. I can't stand Mussolini either."

Once again, I felt proud of my papa.

After primary, I started first grade. I thought Mom would understand when I had the same problem she'd endured about needing supplies, but it returned to visit my generation. My teacher announced we'd be writing on the blue-lined pages of three-ring, loose-leaf notebooks. She gave us instructions to tell our parents what we needed. Mil in second grade, Jerry in fourth, and Lee in fifth received similar directives. At supper, we all conveyed our teachers' requests. "I can't buy four notebooks," Mom said. "I'll buy one of everything for Lee, and the rest of you can share."

"But Mom, we have lessons in four different classrooms," I said.

"Tell the teacher your parents can't afford to buy you that stuff. If she wants you to have it, she can buy it."

At school the next day, the nun asked us to hold up our loose-leaf notebooks. A few of us who didn't have them were scolded, belittled, and given one more day to "remember to bring them in tomorrow."

The second time, scolding and berating weren't enough. The nun walked though the group and whacked us on the knuckles with a yardstick.

"Sister Mary, my mother said she couldn't afford to buy me a notebook."

"That's a lie. I saw your sister walking in the hall with one. While your mother was at the store buying that, she would have bought yours if you had asked her." She smacked my leg with the yardstick. "You're disobedient. You don't care if you fail."

The following day, the exasperated nun sent me to the principal's office for discipline.

"Don't blame your mother," the Superior said. "She's a wonderful lady who works hard and doesn't deserve to have you bad-mouthing her. I'm sure if you'd just explain what you need, she'd get it for you."

I got into a lousy habit of begging my sister for sheets of paper from her notebook. She sighed, clenched her teeth, and grumbled, "Go ahead and take some."

Poor Lee would find herself in that position many times over several years. Mom would buy her school supplies, toys, and clothes but nothing for me. "It's yours, Lee, but share it with your siblings. I can't afford to get four of everything." The first time I'd ever have a garment that wasn't a faded, often-re-hemmed, outgrown hand-me-down of Lee's was when she stopped growing.

What annoyed yet almost amused me was how the nuns couldn't see the obvious. Lee would walk in wearing brand-new white blouses and navy-blue skirts, our school uniform. I'd show up in ill-fitting outfits that almost begged to join the dust rag pile.

"Why can't you dress nice, like your sister?" the nuns asked. "Look how neat she looks. Why do you always look so messy, when you live in the same house? If you took better care of your clothes, you'd look just as neat. You should be ashamed to be seen in public like that."

I was.

Chapter 9

WHEN MAMA PRAYED

THIS STORY WON'T resemble the typical memoirs of a mother in prayer. If I said, "My old-world Sicilian mother prayed," most people would envision rosary beads, head bowed in reverence, and teary eyes. But there was nothing typical about my mother. She followed her own mode of doing things.

When World War II broke out, my oldest brother, Ang, was a marine assigned to the Pacific. Mama's beloved firstborn and her favorite male child, Ang fought in land and sea battles against Japan. Our ships were being sunk, and on shore our infantrymen dodged machine-gun bullets.

If we went to the movies to try to escape the pressures of these worries, the film industry inevitably showed us war stories. Mom insisted she saw Ang in every movie's footage. "Mom, these are Hollywood actors; you couldn't have seen Ang in the picture."

"I know my son when I see him, and I saw him in the movie. These are signs from God that Ang escaped being killed in battle."

At home each night, she'd go into her unique brand of prayer-making deals with God.

"God," she'd shout, "I'll give up using sugar in my coffee until the war ends!"

She called this *"café di penitenza"* (coffee of penance). She could picture angels in heaven approaching the Lord and saying, "Look. That poor woman in New Jersey will continue to inflict suffering upon herself until you end this war."

Sugar had become unattainable during that time. Most Americans and Europeans learned to drink their coffee sugarless; some preferred it that way. But at my young age, who was I to tell Mom what bargains would or wouldn't work between her and God?

Next, she prayed with props. One day she chose an egg. She placed it on the kitchen table and yelled, "God. If the war is going to end in one year, let this egg roll over once."

The egg just sat there. Then, "If the war will end in two years, let this egg roll over twice." Nothing happened.

When she got to twenty-five, I said, "Mama, maybe God doesn't want us to know when the war will end."

She picked it up, broke it, and dropped the white into a tall glass of cold water. It formed a predictable, vertical blob. "Look, those are sails. God is showing me that Ang is sailing back home on a ship. See the ensigns waving in the wind?"

Not a good time, I suppose, to say, "Mama, nowadays U.S. military ships don't have sails."

Next, she slid the yolk into the water. It looked just like an egg yolk in a glass of cold water. "That's forming a parachute. God is telling me that Ang will drop from a plane in a parachute."

Okay, maybe she was nuts.

Toward the end of the war, Ang contracted a touch of malaria and flew home alive and ambulatory. He never met a parachute in his entire life.

Perhaps faith skips a generation. Eventually, my daughter, Joleen, would start drinking a sugar-free soft drink she called *"soda di penitenza."* This would be her bargain with God to end her war with calories.

Outdoors, the biggest menace to our safety was a wolf pack of seventeen-year-olds known as the "Wee-Chee Gang." They embodied the conservatives' best argument for capital punishment, the Calvinists' best argument for mankind's total depravity, and the evangelists' best argument for fire and brimstone.

When that gang roamed the area, we went into every-kid-for-himself mode. Parochial school kids began each school day in church at eight o'clock Mass. When the gang arrived, older siblings, charged with conducting me safely to the church, abandoned their posts without apology and outdistanced me using much longer strides.

The youngest of five latchkey slum kids, I faced challenges. In our section of Paterson, smokestacks from the factories belched pungent black smoke into the air near our tenement flat. If we ran our fingers over the siding of our building, they'd be caked with soot. Factory whistles and train rumblings mixed with loud arguments a few blocks away.

Except for weeds and what was laughingly called our "victory garden"—a dozen anorexic radishes—our yard was devoid of vegetation. World War II brought an acute manpower shortage, eliminating such luxuries as law enforcement and school buses. We walked (or sprinted) the mile to our crumbling church before we could continue to our dilapidated school.

I was tiny for my six years, but had mapped out a strategy of maneuvering behind taller objects. Foul-smelling garbage cans and pieces of industrial debris kept me beyond the enemies' line of vision. It worked well, except for Grouch Lady's privacy fence. This jutted out so that getting around it placed me in plain sight for all of its 150-foot length. She would yell if she caught me trespassing, but the only way to duck the gang was to go through her yard. At each end of her fence, there was a loose board just wide enough for me to squeeze through. I thought that if I could sneak across quickly and quietly, I could escape her detection.

That morning, I risked it. I trespassed. No sooner was I inside her yard than a miniature dust mop with feet sprang up from a fragrant lilac bed and yelped. A second-story window opened. Grouch Lady dumped a pan of frigid water on my swiftly moving little frame. I emerged at the other end of the fence dripping, shivering, and filthy.

I envisioned Sister Mary Neat Freak chiding, "Florence Calderone, you can't come into church like that. March right back home and put on clean clothes. You people can't help being poor, but you have no excuse for being dirty."

As I turned onto Beech Street at Fitzmaurice's Funeral Home, I almost bumped into a grinning, curly-haired, pudgy five-year-old. "You cut through Angelina's yard, didn't you?"

"I would've made it if it hadn't been for that nasty little mutt."

"Tippy's just doing his job."

"Well, watch out. The Wee-Chee Gang is out."

"They'll never come here. They tried it once. I told them all the crates in this yard contain coffins with dead bodies. That scared them off for good."

"They're afraid of dead bodies? That's interesting. I heard they once beat a kid to death in a street fight."

"Yeah, Angelina's son . . . last year. She planted the lilac bed as a shrine to him and nobody's allowed near it. Tippy still pines for him and guards it."

"Oh, how sad!"

He extended his hand to shake mine under the textbooks I carried. "I'm Eddie Fitzmaurice. I don't live here. I live on East 34th Street. But my uncles own this funeral home. You can cut through here anytime you want to dodge the gangs."

"Thanks, Eddie. I'm Florence Calderone."

I proceeded to Mass. The nun did grouch about my appearance, but she had come to expect odd behavior and even odder explanations from me.

Weeks later, Sister Mary had me in an angel costume leading a solemn procession down Beech Street. A voice from Fitzmaurice's balcony shouted, "Hey, Florence. I never saw you when you were dry before. You look great."

I wondered how I'd ever explain that one to a nun who deemed it mortal sin to converse with an unrelated male. Once again, my fears were exaggerated. At least for the time being, the sister let me live.

My meeting Eddie would begin one of the most beautiful platonic friendships I'd ever have with another earthling.

Chapter 10

THE LAMP

WHEN EVERYTHING ELSE you own is secondhand, a new store-bought item becomes treasured. That's how Mom felt about a gaudy china lamp that adorned a shelf in our living room.

I was still six when Mom imposed the edict. "The living room is forbidden territory. Its door is to be kept shut when I'm not home."

Although Lee was assigned to watch me, two days a week choir practice detained her after school. On days when she didn't have choir, she'd hang out with her girlfriends. This left me home with brothers Jerry and Emilio (Mil.)

Before heading to her bus stop each morning, Mom would issue orders. "Jerry and Mil, after school go to Messina's Grocery for tomato paste and pasta so Lee can cook supper. I want to find it ready and on the table when I get home."

"Ma, we can't go there after school," Mil said. "That's where all the rough gangs prowl between three and five o'clock."

Mom had never seen the gangs. They were still sleeping at seven when she left for work and eating supper when she returned at five thirty. "Emilio, learn to get along with people; they tend to treat you the way you treat them." (This gem from the same Maria who'd recount how she'd watched her future brother-in-law stab a man to death in

Casteltermini.) My brothers soon learned that bullying me into running their errands worked better than trying to reason with our mother.

The first time this happened, I sprinted to the corner store. Jerry and Mil headed straight to the untouchable living room to play, roughhouse, and climb all over the furniture. I returned from Messina's Grocery with the items and found the boys running across a sofa in the forbidden area.

"Mom said we're not allowed in the living room."

"Listen, brat, if you squeal, we'll snap your neck in half."

One day I heard a crash. I looked in horror through the living room's open doorway. Mom's precious lamp lay in tiny pieces on the floor. My brothers discussed possible alibis, spotted me, and had their answer. "It's easy," Jerry said. "Let's just say Florence did it. Let her take the beating."

At five thirty, no sooner had Mom entered the house than Jerry and Mil ran to hug her. Almost in unison, they said, "Ma, Florence broke the lamp in the living room. We saw her do it."

"What were you doing in the living room?" Mom asked me. "You know you're not allowed in there."

"I wasn't in the living room, Mama."

"You dirty, rotten liar. You broke my rules and you broke my lamp. Why?"

"Mama, I didn't break your lamp."

She stamped her foot. "How can you deny it? Here are two eyewitnesses who saw you do it."

Nobody asked how I could possibly reach up that high when I was tiny and my older brothers easily outreached me. Then she took out "the stick," a twenty-inch-long wooden one-by-two.

"I'll keep beating you until you admit it. Now, confess that you went into that room and broke my lamp. Beg my forgiveness and promise never to lie again."

After enough blows from the stick, I knew the only way to end this torment was to claim guilt and apologize. Even afterwards, she continued hitting me "to teach me a lesson I'd never forget." I now understood the concept of taking punishment for someone else's wrongdoing.

I received mixed messages regarding Mom's disdain for lies. Wasn't this the same person who'd lied about my age to qualify me for pre-kindergarten? After I had turned six, at times Mom took me along as her language interpreter on errands. Before we'd board the bus, she'd say, "If the driver asks how old you are, tell him you're four. That way I won't have to pay bus fare for you."

Often when my brothers went to movie theaters, she'd urge them to sneak in by the fire exit doors when the show was just beginning. "That's when ushers are distracted with ticket counting and seating people. You won't get caught."

If I said, "Mama, that's the same as lying and stealing," she'd say, "God understands because we're poor. The people who own the movie theater are rich."

The lamp incident established a pattern that would endure for more years than I'd imagine.

Briefly, Mama worked with Marietta Tucci, whom she referred to as an *evangelista*. I never met her, but God would use her to plant a vital seed in my heart—that the Bible is the Word of God. She would often quote Scriptures to Mom, who would bring these quotations home.

"The Bible says not to make any graven images. That's in the Ten Commandments."

Yet at school and mandatory daily morning masses, we were surrounded by sculptures of saints.

"Of course, we don't worship the statues," the nuns said. "We just have them to remind us of the saints we're asking to bring our requests to God."

"Why go through saints, sister? Why can't we just bring our requests straight to God?"

"We could, Florence, but we're not worthy the way the saints are."

One graven image Mama required me to wear was the "miraculous medal." An inch-long oval-shaped hunk of nickel, it bore an engraving of Christ's mother on the front. I considered it a holy good luck charm.

One coworker Mom envied was Josie. She outdid Mom by sewing more pieces, thereby earning more money. Josie also enjoyed boasting about her son's awards at the piano.

When I'd once asked Mom, if I could take singing lessons, she'd said, "If we gave you music lessons, we'd have to let four other kids have them. We can't afford that, and you don't deserve them, anyway."

Later that same month, she bought a violin to start Jerry with lessons, but he soon lost interest and gave up the violin.

"John, I want Lee to have piano lessons."

"Pianos cost a lot of money."

"Why should Josie's kid outdo mine?"

After months of screaming matches, Pop agreed to buy a used upright piano for Lee to study music. The only place it fit in our cluttered, five-room flat was the forbidden living room. "All right, Lee has special permission to enter the living room to practice the piano."

Lee enjoyed the instrument as an occasional toy she played by ear. Within a few weeks, however, lessons and practice became tedious and she quit. Mom then enrolled Mil, who also gave up when the novelty wore off. Desperate to justify their purchase, she started me on lessons when I was six. I determined to learn it well and make my parents proud of me. For six months, I remained faithful in my daily practice sessions.

One afternoon, as I climbed onto the piano bench, my heart groaned at what I saw. Some keys were halfway between down and their normal position. The ivory had been chipped off. I pressed them, but they made no sound. I reached up to slide open the door that covered the keys' hammers and saw splintered wood. Could rodents have damaged it, or were these invaders bipeds?

When Mom arrived home, my worst suspicions were soon confirmed.

"Ma, Mil and I saw Florence break the piano," Jerry said. Mil nodded. Mom stamped her foot and waved clenched fists toward me. "How could you do this? Why did you do this? I could kill you right now. You know how much that piano meant to me."

I burst into tears. "Mama, I didn't break it. I like the piano and I want to learn it. I found it broken when I got home."

Behind her I could see my brothers holding their hands over their mouths, stifling laughs. Again, Mom reached for the stick. "I'll keep beating you until you admit you broke the piano, beg forgiveness, and promise never to lie again."

THE LAMP

Trying to convince her otherwise was like combing my hair in a hurricane. And if I could persuade her, I'd be in for a pummeling from the true culprits the next day. I took the rap and the humiliation.

In those days, battered children were patched up in hospital emergency rooms and sent right back home. In my case, unless neighbors reported my injuries, nobody took me to an emergency room. The term "battered child syndrome" wasn't coined until decades later.

One evening that year I was jostled off a staircase landing. I plunged down eighteen steps, slamming my forehead against a steel doorplate below.

"Maria, I'll take her to the hospital," Pop said.

"No, John. The hospital workers will think I'm a bad mother. I'll cure her myself."

"Ha, ha, you look like Frankenstein's monster," my brothers said.

The impact had fractured my skull. Eventually, the swelling on my nose and forehead went down. But my reading skills plunged to the fifth percentile.

Up 'til then, nobody had ever bought toys for me. Even Toto's lavish gifts consisted entirely of women's jewelry. But occasionally Pop rummaged among people's cast-offs and found objects from which he'd make playthings. Our flat occupied the second story of a run-down old two-family house. Its tiny backyard abutted the rear wall of a warehouse. Using chains and wood scraps, Pop made me a swing, which I shared with my siblings. At times, Pop would hollow out apricot pits and poke holes in them to produce shrill-sounding whistles. The apricot-pit whistle typified the crafts young boys mastered in Sicily.

My eighth summer, late in August, he cobbled together a small structure at the far end of the yard. It stood about four feet by six feet square and five feet high with a small glass window at one end and a door at the other. The "rug" on the floor was a large straw mat someone had discarded. Pop came into the house, took my hand, and escorted me to the yard.

"Let me show you the new playhouse your papa just finished making for you. See, I even installed a metal doorbell. You turn this key and it rings."

I tested the bell, squealed with delight, and gave him a big hug. Then he left for his afternoon work shift.

As Pop rounded the corner to his bus stop, Jerry and Mil came outside and surveyed the structure.

"What's this stupid-looking thing?" Jerry said.

"It's my playhouse that Papa built."

"Hey, this'll make a neat clubhouse for us and our buddies. Okay, brat, out! No girls allowed in our fort."

"When did it become your fort? Papa made it for me."

"We just outvoted you." They shoved me to the side. I started crying.

"Can't we share it or take turns using it?"

"Nope. You lose. And if you ever tell anybody, we'll pick up the pieces of your bones with a dishrag."

If I have any feminist leanings today, the "no girls allowed" statement launched them. I accepted defeat and didn't tell Pop that I never got to enter or use my playhouse.

Late one afternoon, instead of the playhouse, I spied a pile of charred boards amid a plume of smoke. Someone had played with matches, set the straw mat afire, and destroyed the little building.

"Pop will kill us when he finds this," Mil said. "We're dead . . . "

Then Jerry spotted me. "Wait a minute, Mil. What are we worrying about? Whose playhouse is this? When in doubt, you know who to blame. Florence is automatically guilty until proven innocent."

When Mom arrived home, the sham commenced. "We found Florence playing with matches in her playhouse," Mil said.

"Yeah, we saw her set fire to the floor mat, so we pulled her out," Jerry said. "That's how come our clothes smell like smoke and ashes."

Nobody asked, "If Florence was in a burning playhouse, why isn't the smell of smoke or ashes on her clothes?"

The usual routine ensued—threats, condemnation without trial, severe beating, forced confession, begging forgiveness, and a humiliating aftermath.

"Your darling little brat repaid you for all your hard work by deliberately and maliciously burning it to the ground," Mom later told Pop. "I have two credible eyewitnesses. Jerry and Mil pulled her from the fire, and she admitted guilt."

Okay, I had "admitted guilt" and had groveled for forgiveness, but where was that forgiveness?

Pop didn't ask me whether I'd started the fire or why. He made no effort to punish or scold me. From then on, he usually just looked away when I was around. He no longer took me to museums, libraries, cathedrals, or Italian movies. No more "Where's Papa's sweet little girl?" when he entered a room to hug me. No more hugs. On Sunday mornings, he'd now attend ten o'clock Mass alone. I'd go at nine o'clock with Lee. The nuns would conscript me to sing masses in Latin with the children's choir.

Pop never made another toy for me, but he did soon make a scooter for my brother Mil.

Standing, Lee, Jerry, and Mil. Florence seated

Occasionally, Mom's only full-blood brother, Uncle Tommy, would stop by while Mom and Pop were at work. I suspect that Mom had told him about Toto, and Tommy was making sure his half brother stayed away when adults weren't around. Now a banquet chef, Tommy worked evenings and weekends, allowing him to be home by day. One afternoon when I was nine, Tommy dropped in to find the boys and me at home squabbling.

"Where's Lee? Your mother said Lee's supposed to be watching you and starting supper."

"She's at her girlfriend's house. She goes there after choir practice to escape us."

"Florence, your Uncle Tommy's going to teach you how to cook the meals your mom likes."

Supper was ready to serve when our exhausted Mom got home. From that day on, I'd cook all the suppers on weekdays. Mom assumed Lee had done it, praised her for it, and assigned me the clean-up tasks after meals.

One special afternoon, Uncle Tommy got married in a small ceremony at his bride's parents' house. Besides our immediate family and hers, the only other guests were Tommy's stepparents, Salvatore Ventura and Miluzza. I recall Ventura as someone I'd seen a thousand times without ever having seen him smile. The only thing I can ever remember his saying to me was "Florenza, why you no make fat?"

Ventura, Milluza, Pop, Mom, Jerry, Tommy, Lee, Mil, and Florence surround bride, Francis

Chapter 11

THE GLASS DOOR PANE

I WAS TEN when my parents bought a left and right duplex house in a slightly classier slum on East 28th Street. Like our previous area, this was also zoned for heavy industrial. We still faced the sellers' bigotry against Italian immigrants, and that made it difficult to buy homes in better areas.

Mom and Pop took me out of classes that morning to interpret for them at the closing.

"That'll be $500 for the down payment, Mr. and Mrs. Calderone," the bank's attorney said. When I relayed the sentence in Sicilian, Mom opened her purse, and pulled out a stack of U.S. savings bonds. Purchased over a ten-year period, their values varied to reflect accrued interest. She signed all twenty and handed them to their lawyer. Mom instructed me to explain the sum exceeded $500, and the excess should apply to their first month's payment.

"Now you're homeowners and landlords," the attorney said. "The rent you'll collect from the other apartment in this two-family house should meet your mortgage payments for you."

"That's what we're counting on," Mom said.

In the new neighborhood, I now walked eleven blocks past trucking warehouses and lumberyards to a public school. But, thank God, there was no Wee-Chee Gang.

The first school day, I crossed East 34th Street, when a voice called out my name. There stood Eddie Fitzmaurice. Now living next to him was Angelina, complete with transplanted flowerbed shrine and pining Tippy. Eddie introduced me to friends on his block. For several years, I'd play hide-and-seek with him, Jim, and Joni. We respected and avoided Angelina's property.

In this school, my art teacher would often hold up my drawings as examples for the class. Whenever she needed a student's picture for a special occasion, she'd ask me to draw it.

Once she selected three paintings from students in grades five to eight and sent them to a statewide contest in Trenton. Two weeks later, the teacher congratulated me and presented me with a red ribbon. "Take this home and show your parents tonight. They'll be so proud of you. Your painting took second prize out of thousands of entries at the State Capitol. As a fifth grader, you even outscored eighth graders."

"Mom, look, I won this," I said when she walked in. "It's the second prize in a state art contest."

She frowned, shrugged, and shook her head in disbelief. "Why didn't that art teacher send one of your brother's paintings? Mil's would've won the first prize."

Culled from among the same student body's efforts, Mil's work had already been considered and eliminated. I walked over to the garbage can, tossed in the prize thousands of kids had coveted, and set the supper table as usual. The next time Pop emptied the garbage container, he pulled out the ribbon.

"What's this thing, Maria?"

"It's nothing, John. Put it back in the garbage."

No longer in choir with my sister or watched by older siblings, I grew more independent. Barbara, a nine-year-old neighbor, attended a Bible class after school. The leader, Mrs. Bulmer, awarded buttons reading, "I brought someone" as incentives for kids to invite friends. Barbara invited me.

The classes had originally taken place in Mrs. Bulmer's living room. Soon, membership rolls swelled to numbers too large for the home. Meetings moved to a church basement. The church? Once again, the same one the caregivers from my original day nursery attended. The walking distance tripled, but I made the transition and kept it secret from my parents for fear they'd stop me from hearing God's Word.

I knew of Jesus, but had been trained to think of him as the "head Saint" among many to whom we might pray. I had heard that he had died on the cross and risen again, but I hadn't grasped the concept of vicarious atonement. Before that, no one had told me that Jesus loved me. Yet, I knew it because I'd once met him as a preschooler in a vivid dream. In the dream, Lee, Mom, and I were at the altar rail of Saint Anthony's. Before us stood a life-sized crucifix. My sister and mother gabbed, ignoring me, while I stared at the crucified stone image. Suddenly, it became living flesh. Christ flew down and embraced me to his chest. Then he stretched his arms out again, flew backward, and resumed his still form on the cross. "Mama, Lee, did you see that? Jesus flew to me and hugged me. Jesus loves me." Lee and Mom dismissed me as "imagining things that never happened." Decades later, I'd memorialize that moment in a song, "Nail-Pierced Hands."

Barbara's family abruptly returned to their native Pennsylvania. Although family health problems forced Mrs. Bulmer to discontinue the Bible class, God knows how to plant seeds he will eventually water.

One feature I'd come to like in our new house was the door that led from the kitchen into the backyard. Its two rectangular, vertical glass panes on the upper half and all wood on the bottom half struck me as vulnerable. Anyone with a good glass cutter could easily break through to the deadbolt lock. We kept shades over windows and door panes. We would lower the shade when we turned the kitchen lights on at dusk.

When the lamp, piano, and playhouse incidents had occurred, no adults had been present. Whatever had transpired became the boys' word against mine. But this Saturday morning could have been different and should have altered all former injustices. As I washed dishes, Mom stood between me and my brothers, who were roughhousing near the back door. Jerry accidentally toppled a chair that struck and shattered a glass pane.

"Uh, oh. What'll we tell Pop, Mil?"

"Silly question. Just tell him Florence did it. They always believe that." He chuckled. "Remember, 'When in doubt, you know who to blame. Florence is guilty until proven innocent.'"

Jerry cleared his throat. His eyes darted toward Mom standing three feet behind Mil. Mil winced and slapped his hand over his mouth. I stifled a laugh.

Finally, the truth came bursting out. Mom's "credible eyewitnesses" just destroyed their own credibility.

Mom clearly heard them, moved the offending chair back to its place at the kitchen table, and collected the shattered pieces of glass. "I know what we'll do," she said. "Let's tell your father I was mopping and accidentally hit the glass with the mop handle. That way he'll get annoyed with me, but he won't punish you guys."

When Pop came home, I overheard Mom's convincing account of "her mishap with the mop handle." He took her word for it, grumbled, but within two days replaced the pane. A few years later, that pane of glass would figure in God's plan for me.

Chapter 12 ✑

MY FIRST PROPOSAL

MOM'S SECOND COUSIN wrote from Casteltermini, requesting a picture of Lee. Instead of sending him one of Lee, Mom found one of me at age eleven and mailed it to him. I handed Mom the letter I'd retrieved from the mailbox the day she received her relative's reaction. He claimed that his son had fallen for me "to the point of folly" and longed to marry me someday.

The reason Mom wouldn't send him Lee's photo soon surfaced. The son dreamed of a future in America. Immigration quotas involved long, complicated wait lists and regulations. The simplest way to bypass these rules was to marry an American citizen. This conferred almost automatic citizenship upon the groom.

"I suspected he was up to something," Mom said. "I never imagined he'd fake an interest in you, though."

"Mom, if I ever receive a marriage proposal, I want it to be genuine and for love, not for a shortcut to citizenship."

"Hah! You should grab onto any offer you can get. Your sister will have the genuine proposals someday. You watch—she'll get a dozen invitations to her senior prom. But with the Calderone family's looks and traits, who'd ever want to court you?"

Before the immigration laws changed, so many men tried to invoke the quota loophole that I lost count of the "visa proposals" I received.

Some would even say, "You could stay married to me just long enough to get my citizenship. Then, under American law, if you don't like me, we can always get a divorce."

I turned them all down. I can be such a heartless creep at times.

Shortly after I turned thirteen, Mom mentioned something I'd hoped she'd forgotten. "You're overdue to have your confirmation in the church. You'll have to do this, but don't expect a party or any gifts."

"Why do I have to be confirmed, Mom?"

"If you don't, the relatives and the *paisani* will think ill of me. And you'd never be able to get married in the church."

"Why would I have to get married in the church?"

"Someday, if some idiot is crazy enough to want you, you might marry a guy who expects a church wedding."

"To be confirmed, I need a sponsor, another godparent. What do you suggest I do about that?"

The sanctity of the godparent/co-parent/Saint John bind kicked in. Technically, the custom called for Mom as co-mother to phone Grace, the other co-mother, but Mom still hadn't resumed speaking to Grace.

"We made a pact. If we broke it, Saint John could get upset and cause us harm. Phone Grace Lobo and ask her to be your sponsor."

Times had changed enough so that most people in Paterson now had telephones. Since it cost more to have an unpublished number, most listings could be found in the directory. I looked her up, located her at a new address in Paterson, and made a call in Sicilian.

"Comare Grace? This is Florence Calderone. To honor Saint John, would you stand up for me at my confirmation?"

"Florence? Giovanni and Maria's daughter?" There was a twenty-second pause. "Out of due respect to Saint John, I'll be honored to be your sponsor if that's what you want. When, where, and what time?"

"I'll get back to you when all that is determined, Comare Grace. Thank you."

A few minutes later, her daughter, Millie, phoned me back. "Florence, how come after all this time you called?"

"Our parents made a deal years ago, Millie. My mother would baptize you, and your mother would confirm me. There's something in Sicilian Catholicism about not offending Saint John the Baptist."

"But why haven't they spoken to us in ten years?"

I related the saga of the failed furniture purchase and how Mom had assumed the bad reference came from her parents.

"Oh, brother! I would have known if anybody asked my parents about yours. Mine would never have said that."

We laughed at the mutual cultural eccentricities that were part of our generation gaps. "They don't have to make sense, Millie."

"Yeah, you're right, Florence. My mother insists that our dreams are messages from God."

"You mean, we're all like Joseph from the Bible story?"

"That's what she'll base life decisions on. When she dreamed I got hurt at the skating rink, I couldn't go skating anymore."

"Millie, I remember when your mom dreamed you were drowning. You were never allowed to go to a swimming pool after that."

"Yeah, I'm amazed that she lets me put water in the bathtub."

God used my confirmation to heal this rift in a family friendship. Even though Mom never offered apologies, Joe and Grace soon acted as though there'd never been a gap in their relationship. Within months, Grace became Mom's coworker and closest friend at the coat factory in Passaic.

Chapter 13

MY AWARD

HOW DID I ever manage it? At age fourteen, I received a silver medal awarded by New York City for swimming prowess. Yet I'd never learned to swim. I didn't win the medal, Ernie did. He gave it to me the way a cadet might give a frat pin to his best girl.

This wasn't supposed to happen to me, the unattractive member of my family. Two inches taller, with model face and figure, my sister Lee heard constant predictions of "Wait until Lee starts high school. She'll break so many hearts. That phone will never stop ringing."

I had inherited Pop's disproportionate features—high forehead; more nose than necessary; small mouth; low, tiny chin. When Marilyn Monroe reigned as the criterion for figures, I was built like a starved version of gymnast Olga Korbut.

I further complicated matters by hanging out with classmate Joni, who looked like the typical cheerleader. Whenever we'd first meet a boy, the moment would come. "Florence, can I talk to you alone a minute?" Then, "Can you give me Joni's phone number?"

That June day Joni, our classmate Jane, and I had discount tickets to Palisades Amusement Park across the Hudson River from Manhattan. Although the attractions usually cost twenty-five cents each, our bargain coupons offered, "Any ten rides for $1." Too young to drive, we traveled to the amusement park by bus.

As we stepped off the "Tilt-a-Whirl," Joni turned ashen. Two courteous, male teens approached and offered to help us find the first-aid station. Since the Palisades usually hired teenage boys, I thought they were park employees. Though Joni soon felt better, the boys continued shadowing us. On "The Hurricane," a voice behind me said, "Not that this ride is dangerous, but is your life insurance paid up?"

I turned around and found myself looking into a pair of iridescent eyes. These eyes could look blue when he wore a blue shirt but turn green or grayish when he wore one of those colors. He flashed a gentle smile. I took my first close look at one of the two who'd been tailing us. He had gleaming, medium-brown hair that dipped into a wave over his sun-bronzed forehead.

"We're vacationing in Manhattan," he said, "but we live in Tampa, Florida. That hurricane ride reminds me of the storms that slam our state in late summer."

"I've read about Florida hurricanes, but I've never been more than fifteen miles from Paterson."

Wherever we went, they'd turn up around the same ride or attraction, and they'd keep up the friendly conversation. When they dared us to venture onto the giant roller coaster, I resisted at first. Later, I spent the rest of my tickets for more rides on it.

At 5:00 PM, the girls and I headed out the front gate to the bus-boarding platform. Iridescent Eyes followed, tapped me on the shoulder, and said, "Can I see you a minute in private?"

I anticipated the usual request for Joni's phone number and stepped aside with him.

"Look, I know this is kind of forward. I mean, we just met and all, but could I have your phone number?"

"You want *my* phone number?"

"Yes. I know you don't even know my name, but . . ."

I noticed my bus slowing for a stop; I'd have to make a quick judgment call. I fumbled through my wallet, found a typewritten identification card, and handed it to him. He scanned and pocketed it. "By the way, Florence, my name is Ernie."

My bus halted and began to fill with passengers. "I'd better run before this bus turns into a pumpkin. So long, Ernie. Nice meeting you."

76

"Thanks. Call you soon."

"Well, did you give him my phone number?" Joni said, giggling, as I waved to Ernie from the bus window.

"No, Joni, I didn't."

Her nostrils flared. "You didn't? Why not? He's so gorgeous."

"He asked for *my* phone number."

Joni's eyes narrowed and her mouth dropped. "And you gave it to him? You're a fool, Flo. A guy you just picked up at an amusement park will never call you."

"He can't call without the number. Besides, I didn't exactly pick him up. I thought he worked for the park."

"Oh, like that makes everything respectable. You wouldn't pick up a stranger, but it's okay if he works there."

"What should I have done if he'd asked for your phone number, Joni? What would you have done?"

Joni turned away and didn't answer.

Early that evening, Ernie did call. "I'm going back to Florida in a few days. I want to see you before I go."

The next afternoon at Paterson's bus terminal, I greeted a pair of almost-navy blue eyes above a Hawaiian shirt and that sparkling smile. "I have good news. We're not going back to Tampa. We're staying in Manhattan."

Then Ernie showed me the prize silver medal he'd won in his swimming tournament. About the diameter of a penny, it had a pin in the back so it could be attached to a collar.

"Wow! Congratulations, Ernie."

"You can have it."

I thanked him and pinned it to my collar.

I took Ernie on a tour of the sights in my hometown. He noticed a skating rink/bowling alley four blocks from my house and a public swimming pool ten blocks farther. At the bus stop when our first date ended, he said, "There's something I want to ask you." He looked around, took a deep breath, and said, "Will you be my girl?"

"Sure."

That summer he met the definition of the ideal boyfriend. Respectful, attentive, smart, and considerate. He phoned often, took me to rinks, parks, and movies. He wrote me poems and sweet letters.

That month a door-to-door salesman came to the house on weekday evenings while Pop was at work. The peddler carried a line of products from clothing to appliances on easy payment terms. Mom wanted a TV set, but she knew Pop wouldn't approve of spending the money. She bought one from the vendor on the installment plan and gathered us kids together to instruct us. "Don't tell your father I bought this set. If he asks where it came from, say Jerry won it in a raffle at school, understand?"

So we had our black-and-white, nineteen-inch, console television, along with our misguided message that it's okay to lie to Pop but never to Mom.

Pop enjoyed watching excerpts of his favorite arias from the New York Metropolitan Opera House on Sunday afternoons.

Ernie and I would occasionally sit and watch TV programs that summer. Out of work at the time, Lee was always somewhere in the house to serve as an inconspicuous chaperone.

When the chilly autumn winds arrived, geographical inconvenience made Ernie's commute impractical. One day, an hour after he'd gone home, the phone rang.

"Is my son, Ernest, there?"

"No, he left about an hour ago."

"It takes more than an hour to get to Manhattan from there? Oh, with the rough gangs and everything around, I get so nervous."

I knew what was coming. Ernie stopped calling. Although I knew his phone number, I wouldn't call him. Back then, it would have seemed too pushy.

The following summer, he returned. Now several inches taller, he wore his hair cropped shorter. My favorite feature, the wave, was gone. An olive-drab T-shirt dulled his eye color. I hoped he would explain his sudden disappearance of a year ago, but he didn't. I'd gotten over the emotional hurt of his abandonment and wouldn't risk its recurrence.

I think God had allowed Ernie into my life to give me this reas-surance: not everyone thought I was as hideous and obnoxious as my mother implied. I also didn't need to live in dread of socializing with males. Not many intended to attack me as my godfather had or belittle me and order me around as my brothers might.

I should have returned it. If I'd known I wouldn't be seeing him again, I might have. But I still cherish "winning" a now-tarnished silver medal that sits inside its original box in my nightstand.

God used the TV set to reintroduce music into my life. One redhead, wielding one tiny instrument, virtually changed the course of musical art to my generation. Arthur Godfrey dominated the airwaves with his *Talent Scouts* and other variety shows. A frequent vacationer in Hawaii, he brought back the ukulele and presented an after-school television series of uke instructions from New York.

An unprecedented spike in uke sales resulted. Kids from six to sixteen compared ridges in their fingers after they'd practiced strumming. When my brother Mil received a uke, we'd both watch and learn from Godfrey. Many uke students would eventually graduate to its six-string big brother, the guitar, and that caused its sales to soar.

The following year, Mil returned from working as a summer camp counselor with a thrift-shop acoustic guitar, to which a fellow-counselor had introduced him. Mil sang and accompanied his rich, baritone voice with guitar chords he'd learned. Then he taught them to me. In time, I resumed reading notes and playing musical instruments. God is so generous.

Part 3

REBELLIOUS, HECTIC
TEEN YEARS

Chapter 14

FIRST AID,
MRS. COOPER STYLE

THE EVENTS IN Mrs. Cooper's class took place before I had repented of all my sins. I probably wouldn't behave like this today.

A huge obstacle to high school graduation in the late 1950s was First Aid class. We had to take it, and too many kids didn't take it seriously enough. They failed the class. Among its casualties were two of my siblings. This alerted me to avoid their mistakes.

What was so hard about it? The concept sounded like a no-brainer. Either we could correctly tie some silly muslin triangle we'd probably never use, or we couldn't. But the teacher worried. If tourniquets were too tight, they could cause gangrene. If too loose, they wouldn't prevent snake venom from reaching the victims' brains—or do whatever tourniquets were supposed to do in those days.

First Aid alternated with Gym, meaning 120 sophomore girls at Gym class one day squeezed into a tiny, disorganized health classroom the next. For the first several minutes, the instructor demonstrated how to tie a certain bandage. Then we'd each team up with a classmate and take turns bandaging and being bandaged. The person putting on the bandage took her victim to the teacher's desk to be graded. Upon passing, she'd become the "injured," and the grading process resumed. In a forty-minute class period with sixty teams of people at various stages of interchangeable bandaging, lining up, and being graded, things became hectic. We had to succeed early in the process, or time ran out, and we scored zero. Enough zeroes meant we'd flunk the course and have to keep retaking it until we passed it.

At the first session, I watched Mrs. Cooper tie an elbow sling. Then I bandaged teammate Joni, and we stood in line. "Not neat enough," Mrs. Cooper said. "Go redo it."

I undid it, retied it, and returned for inspection.

"Is it better this time, Mrs. Cooper?"

"Yes, much better. You have an A."

Classmate Winnie saw me leaving Mrs. Cooper's desk with my successfully bandaged victim. Well hidden in the back of the room, she whispered, "Florence, yours passed? Before you untie that, let me borrow it."

But when Winnie reached the front with the same work that had just received an A, Mrs. Cooper said, "That's too sloppy, Winifred. Try again."

I observed Mrs. Cooper for several minutes and noticed a pattern. "This teacher consistently disapproves every first attempt but approves the second one. Winnie, try getting right back in line with that same bandage and saying, 'Now is this okay, Mrs. Cooper?'"

With time growing short and Joni still needing her turn to bandage me, Winnie followed my suggestion. It worked.

At the next class session, the teacher chose me as her demonstration model. After she wrapped my forehead, she sent me off to do likewise for my victim.

"Wait, don't undo that yet," Joni said. "I'll use it."

Joni got in line, and took Mrs. Cooper's own meticulous work to her for grading.

"That's much too tight," Mrs. Cooper said. "Try it again."

Joni recalled what had worked the previous time for Winnie and tried the same ploy. This time Mrs. Cooper declared the undisturbed bandage "perfect."

After that, I'd bandage Joni for whatever the injury was and get in line with it once. Upon arriving at the grading desk, I'd smile and say, "Is this neat enough now, Mrs. Cooper?"

"Yes, much neater," the harried teacher would reply and give me an A.

So I aced First Aid on my first try and won the certificate attesting to my outstanding qualifications. Please hope that if you're ever injured, I'm not the only one around to bandage you.

Friends Frank, Joni, Lou, and Artie at Westside Park

Chapter 15 ❧

BATHWATER

CONSIDERED LUXURIES IN the mid-1950s, multiple bathrooms, automatic hot water heaters and shower fixtures didn't exist in our home. Before each bath, we'd hold a lit match to some jets, turn on the gas, shut the heater door, and wait. In an hour, this contraption would warm enough water to fill the claw-foot bathtub halfway.

Never expected to clean up after themselves, my brothers didn't scrub their bathtub rings of dirty dead skin after bathing. That annoying task fell to the next bather.

By then Ang had married and started a family, on the West Coast. I was the youngest of four teenagers still at home. On weekdays we'd manage with hasty morning sponge baths, but on weekend date nights we'd all bathe within a span of a few hours. Since we couldn't all bathe if we started too close to date time, I dodged the last-minute rush. Around 1:00 PM I'd heat water, scrub the tub, and then fill it for a quick bath.

My sixteen-year-old brother, Mil, had it timed perfectly. The moment I had the tub filled, he'd yell, "Wait a second; don't lock that door yet; I have to go." He'd enter the bathroom, lock me out, strip, and then climb into my warm, welcoming bathwater.

I didn't trust Mil the way Charlie Brown trusts Lucy to hold the football for him to kick, so I'd try to keep him out of the bathroom.

But Mom would say, "Let him use the bathroom. You want his bladder to burst?"

Week after week, I'd have to reheat water, re-scrub, and then refill the bathtub. If I gave advance notice and the tub wasn't filled yet, nobody had to go. If I said, "I don't trust you. You just want to use my bathwater," Mom inevitably forced my hand and let him swipe my bath rights every time.

If I had been the mother, I'd have said, "Mil, you gave your word, and you lied to your sister. Wait your turn. Prepare your own bath." But in our culture, because he was older and male, Mil reigned as the superior party. By not feeling obligated to prepare and draw his baths first, I was considered the selfish one.

One day I reached my threshold of fiendishness. After I heated the water, scrubbed, and filled the tub as usual, right on cue, Mil knocked on the door with his predictable need. He wasn't expecting what happened next. There it sat, still in its original gift box on a shelf—my Christmas present from classmate Bobby Turndorf. The four-ounce bottle of Chanel No. 5 perfume dared me. I dumped it all into the water. Its flowery fragrance gradually began sneaking in to fill the small room. How sweet, delicate, and feminine!

"Mil, I'll open this door if you solemnly promise you won't set foot into the bathtub."

"I swear I won't touch your bathwater."

In my chenille robe, I stepped outside to let him in. I heard *click*, then *splash*, then, "What the . . . ? Who put perfume in my bathwater?"

"It's *my* bathwater; you just swore you wouldn't use it."

Clad only with a bath towel around his waist, Mil charged out, waving clenched fists. But this gain was well worth the pain he'd inflicted on me. After that, my preparations for Saturday dates were much more peaceful. Never again did anyone try to usurp my delicately scented bathwater.

Chapter 16 〜

MY WORST DAY

"I will strengthen you, though you have not acknowledged me."
—Isaiah 45:5b (NIV).

THE BIBLE SAYS the Devil is the author of confusion. But this time I believe God allowed what transpired so he could later use it for his glory. The autumn I turned fifteen, my sister, Lee, now nineteen, worked as an office receptionist. Brother Mil was in eleventh grade, and Jerry had completed high school and joined the navy.

A series of virtually unprecedented events occurred that day. First, Mom happened to be at home on a weekday. Because she received no money for staying home, only her burst appendix and the house purchase had ever kept her from the factory. Even when I had fractured my skull at age six, she'd said, "I can't forfeit eight hours' wages. Don't open the door to anybody. Your guardian angel will watch you."

But on this particular Tuesday in October, Mom's employer had a death in his family and closed the shop.

"Mom, I have drama club rehearsal after school until 5:00 PM, so I'll be home about 5:30," I said before heading out that morning. I walked to school with brother Mil. At 2:30, I attended rehearsal and then headed home at 5.

When I entered the house, Mom, Lee, and Mil stood glaring with arms folded. "Where have you been?" Mom said.

"In school, at rehearsal. Remember, I told you this morning . . ."

"No, you weren't in school, you lying, streetwalking slut. Where were you really?"

"What makes you think I wasn't in school?"

"You mean, how do I know? Your friend Joni, who's also in the drama club play, phoned here at 4:30 asking for you. If there'd really been a rehearsal, Joni would've been there too."

She indicated the directory next to the telephone. "To make sure I was right, I even called your school, and nobody answered. Nobody was in the building. There was no rehearsal."

"Mom, Joni has a bit part—seven lines in act 3. We rehearsed acts 1 and 2 today. She didn't need to be there. Nobody answered because the school's switchboard closes at four o'clock when the office staff leaves."

"If you were really there, why didn't you answer it?"

"Rehearsals are in the auditorium. Phones ring in the office, where we can't hear them from the stage."

"Unless you admit the truth immediately, I'll give you the worst punishment of your life."

I hurried to the phone directory, looked up the drama teacher's home phone number, and dialed it. "Miss George, this is Florence Calderone. Would you please tell my mother where I was today? She won't believe me and plans to punish me."

I handed the phone to Mom.

"Florence was with me at drama rehearsal in the school auditorium from 2:30 until 5:00 PM today," Miss George said.

Mom thanked her and hung up.

"Oh, that teacher would lie for you because you're such a brownie," Mil said. "My track coach always says we're at track practice when we cut classes."

The double standard irritated me. Mil had just admitted cutting classes, and nobody cared why or even asked where he'd really been. Why would it matter? Boys couldn't get pregnant and disgrace the family name that way.

Now Mom escalated her push for "the truth." Meanwhile, I felt hungry and went to the kitchen to look for groceries I had bought the previous day to cook for supper. That week, Pop worked the 2:00 PM to 11:00 PM shift. Lee and Mil sat down on a couch to watch TV. They had no idea what was about to take place.

Mom followed me into the kitchen and took out the stick. "You'd better confess right now because I won't stop beating you until you do."

By this time in life, I had settled into a routine. Years of browbeating from bigger, older siblings had resigned me to running my brothers' errands and silently watching them take the credit. I cooked suppers and saw my sister garner the praise. I washed the dishes afterward because that was my own daily assigned task. Each evening I'd also scrub one of two hand-me-down outfits and hang it on the bathroom towel rack to dry. The following morning, I'd press the outfit I'd wear to school. Mil would come out of his room and order me to iron a shirt for him.

Most of these things happened while Mom was at work. She didn't know that Uncle Tommy had taught me to cook. She was unaware that Lee had never learned how to use the gas range or that I usually did the supper grocery shopping.

Brandishing the dreaded stick, Mom came at me and swatted at my leg. I darted to one side. The stick slammed against the chrome table leg and smashed into splintered pieces. Now even more infuriated, she dropped what was left of it and started slapping and punching me with both hands. Although an inch shorter than I was, she held a fifty-pound advantage. With years of experience in defending myself in street fights, I scored higher points for agility. My mom had met her match for stubbornness.

Years earlier, I'd caved in under the blows of the stick, but not this time.

"You've always been a rotten liar!" Mom shouted. "Like when you broke my lamp and the piano and set fire to the playhouse. I've always had to beat the truth out of you."

"Mom, I never broke that lamp or the piano. I never burned the playhouse. I took the blame because you wouldn't stop beating me unless I did. If I accused my brothers, they'd have denied it and beaten me up the next day."

My thoughts flashed back to the broken door pane incident of a few years earlier. "Remember when you heard Mil tell Jerry to blame me for breaking the glass in the back door? That time you told Pop you broke it with the mop handle."

"No, I don't recall anything like that. You're making it up. How dare you accuse my sons? You lying tramp, I'll kill you."

I wouldn't strike my mother, but I knew how to intercept a punch. Now I blocked and dodged her fists with what mimicked the speed of a strobe light. She stopped momentarily and sighed in frustration. I thought she had tired or given up, and I let my guard down. Then she seized my neck with both hands and squeezed. I struggled for breath, interlocked the fingers of both my hands together, and thrust them upward between her forearms. That action sent her hands flying apart.

Again, she stopped. Again, thinking the matter closed, I let my guard down. With my back to her, I opened the cutlery drawer in the middle of the table to begin preparing supper. Mom lunged past my arm and snatched a cook's knife that had a six-inch blade. She spun me around and held me down against the table. Then she pressed the blade into my throat with a horizontal sawing action.

"You can't disgrace me anymore you filthy liar. I'll get rid of you forever, toss your corpse into the alley, and tell the police the street gangs did it."

Pinned on my back under her body weight, I pushed my fingers up against the blade. Although the knife cut my fingers, I kept it from severing the carotid artery. Weakened from the pain, certain I couldn't keep up the fight any longer, I screamed, "God, help me!"

No sooner had the words left my lips when he replied with a miracle—a knock on the kitchen door. Mom stopped, straightened, bolted to the sink with the knife, washed the blood off, and returned it to the drawer. I spun around to look at the door's transparent pane and saw Mrs. Galski,* our next-door neighbor peering in.

Here three more unusual circumstances converged. All our window shades, normally lowered when the kitchen lights went on, remained in their up position. Across the narrow driveway from her kitchen, Mrs. Galski had observed what was happening. Usually her husband repaired car bodies in his garage shop nearby, his drills and sanders drowning out any surrounding noises. This day, however, they stayed silent. His wife had heard our shouting match. Mrs. Galski had never come to our house before. Mom's full-time work schedule and thick accent made friendship and communication between them impractical. But God sent Mrs. Galski at that moment to rescue me.

I went to the door and opened it. "Hi, Mrs. Galski. Come on in."

She froze wide-eyed and whispered, "Did I just see what I think I saw?"

I surveyed my bleeding fingers and nodded. "Yeah, my mother just tried to slit my throat."

The horrified neighbor backpedaled and scurried home. Yet I felt safety and relief. Because the combined testimony of a neighbor and a drama teacher could incriminate her, Mom wouldn't dare kill me now—or so I thought. I went to the bathroom sink and ran cold water on my cuts. Then, with hands now wrapped in gauze and adhesive tape, I proceeded to cook pasta and tomato sauce. I set the table and doled out the portions on everyone's plate.

Per Sicilian custom, the cook serves others first, herself last. But she takes the first bite to establish trust that the food isn't poisoned.

When I sat down to eat, Mom shot to her feet, seized my dish, and dashed to the garbage can. She dumped the plate's entire contents and told my sister, "Tell that slut that she'll never taste another morsel until she admits where she really was today. She doesn't deserve to be in my house or to eat at my table."

I ran upstairs to the bedroom I shared with my sister and cried. In the mirror, I viewed the damage to my neck. I spotted the bloodied chain holding the "miraculous medal" I'd worn since age six to please my mother. I lifted it off and tossed it into the wastebasket.

After supper, I heard Mom and my siblings downstairs reciting their nightly Rosary in Italian. Fifty Ave Marias, five Pater Nostri, and one Gloria Patri droned by rote, an appropriate backdrop to camouflage the bloodshed of seventy minutes earlier. Then my sister, Lee, came up to the room. "You really messed up this time. Mom is furious with you."

I examined the bloodstained bandages on my fingers. "No kidding."

"Why don't you just admit where you were, apologize, and get it over with?"

I could almost understand why Mom might be confused. She wouldn't know the layout of an American high school, but Lee and Mil could see how a phone ringing in the office wasn't audible from the auditorium's stage down the hall. They could verify that at 4:00 PM the school office door was locked. Never having been in drama club plays, however, they didn't grasp why cast member Joni wouldn't be at the same rehearsal with me. If I had called Joni and asked her to explain it, they wouldn't have believed her, either. If they thought my drama teacher would lie for me, wouldn't they think the same of my best friend?

"My teacher vouched for the fact that I was in school. Mom doesn't want to believe me. It's Mom's problem."

"You're an incorrigible juvenile delinquent. Mom changed the secret hiding place for the door key, so you'll be locked out. Mil and I aren't allowed to give you access to food or money. She plans to starve you until you confess."

I negated her words by shaking my head. "An incorrigible juvenile delinquent can put a rock through a glass door pane faster than Pop can keep replacing it. Tell Mom there are other drawbacks."

"Like what? What else will you do?"

"It's what I won't do. I won't run errands for others to take the credit. I won't cook meals I can't take part in. I won't wash the dishes from those meals." I noticed I hadn't heard any clatter of china from the sink after they ate. "Who washed tonight's dishes?"

"Nobody yet. They're still on the table. Cleanup and dishes are your jobs."

"I just resigned. And I won't go to Mass with you on Sundays anymore."

"It's a mortal sin to miss Mass unless you're sick."

"Mom's not sick. She never goes to Mass. Why should I?"

"Mom stays home on Sundays to cook dinner."

I bit my lip to keep from laughing. "When I used to go to masses with Pop, we'd get out of church at eleven. Then we'd stop at the chicken store for a hen Mom could start roasting for dinner. She never cooked while we were at Mass."

Before retiring that night, I washed the dress I'd planned to wear the following day and spread it on a towel rack to dry. Next morning, still in nightclothes, I went to get the dress to iron it. I found the only two outfits I owned submerged under three inches of cold water in the bathtub. I reached for the iron on the pantry shelf, where it typically rested when not in use. I touched an empty space.

To prepare my lunch, I looked in the refrigerator. Mother Hubbard's cupboard was better stocked. I surveyed the backyard. Under an oak, sparrows pecked at the last of our bread heels Mom had shredded and flung there.

I went to my sister's part of the closet and groped in its darkness to borrow a blouse and skirt. Since Lee stood two inches taller, the skirt would look a bit too long, but when better is missing, worse improves. I found a flimsy scarf to hide the cuts on my neck. In the dim dawn light, I didn't realize that the scarf I'd chosen was Kelly green, the skirt navy blue, and the blouse pale pink.

Before permanent press fabrics, everything required ironing after being laundered. A yawning Mil came into the kitchen. "Hey, stupid, iron me a shirt."

"Find the iron, and you've got a deal."

"What do you mean? You know where Ma keeps the iron."

"It's not there."

"What am I supposed to do for a shirt? I can't go to school with a wrinkled one."

The school's dress code banned T-shirts and jeans. I almost pitied him for this contingency that Mom hadn't considered. I recalled seeing museum pieces people had used before the invention of electric irons. Years earlier, Pop had told me they heated these rusty hunks of metal on wood stoves. A Pyrex coffee pot sat on our kitchen gas range. If heated right, that might take wrinkles out of fabrics. Not shaped to get around cuffs and buttons, it worked imperfectly—but better was missing.

Mil pulled the shirt on and buttoned it. "I'm not allowed to walk to school with you or even talk to you anymore."

"Fine. Take a head start. I'll go on without you."

When I called, you answered me; you made me bold and stout-hearted.

—Psalm 138:3 (NIV)

95

A scene from *Our Miss Brooks*, the play we were rehearsing that dreadful day until 5:00 PM. Wearing a scarf to hide the cuts, Florence is second from the right.

Mom, Lee, and Pop in driveway across from the Galskis'.

Chapter 17

THE AFTERMATH

Even now my witness is in heaven; my advocate is on high.

—Job 16:19 (NIV)

I PONDERED THE words of the Spanish proverb "Only the pallbearer knows the weight of the corpse." In the school corridor, I slammed my locker door shut. An unfamiliar voice intruded on my thoughts.

"Your blue skirt clashes with the green scarf. That skirt's too long; they're not showing hemlines that far below the knee this fall. And you don't wear a pink blouse in October. It's a spring color."

"Who cares?"

"You should care. You'd be one of the coolest girls in school if only you'd take more pride in your appearance. Let me help you coordinate your wardrobe."

I wondered how she managed to keep her white blouse and anklets so laundry-commercial immaculate between home and school. Her maroon woolen jumper looked as though it had just come from Macy's rack. "What's your name?"

She practically curtseyed. "Mitzy."

"I'm sure you mean well, Mitzy, but I sincerely hope my wardrobe is the worst problem you'll ever face."

"Well, it's not really my problem at all . . ."

"Bingo! I happen to believe two things: True friends accept us for ourselves, not our wardrobes. And people who don't buy our clothes for us shouldn't tell us how to dress."

Poor Mitzy looked like a Good Samaritan who'd just received a subpoena from her beneficiary. Could I tell her I'd groped in a dark closet to commandeer what I thought was a white blouse and a black skirt?

Later, in the school cafeteria, my pal Diana assumed I'd forgotten my lunch. I didn't air our dirty family secrets. They would have made her uncomfortable, and she'd never believe what a madhouse I lived in. I asked Diana if she knew who fashion-plate Mitzy was.

"The ritzy suburb where she lives has no high school yet, so she was assigned here. Her father's an MD. Her mother's a college professor. Mitzy's an only child who got a new, white Cadillac convertible for her birthday. She owns a pet horse named *Savoir Faire*."

I'd see Mitzy again seven years later. After her graduation from Manhattan's prestigious Parsons School of Design, she'd be my waitress at a local roadside diner.

At the end of this school day, I knew I'd be locked out when I returned home. Approaching the kitchen door, I asked God to show me the new hiding place for the latchkey. He led my feet straight to the cellar entrance at the far edge of the house. I wouldn't have thought to look that distance from the kitchen. I opened an outer screen door and glanced down to my right. The key hung on a nail fastened to the cellar doorpost.

On Thursday morning, the third day of my punishment fast, I woke early, trembling and famished. I knew the Lord's Prayer and started to recite it silently. When I got to the part that says, "Give us this day our daily bread," I paused. "Okay, God, about this 'daily bread' thing. I weigh eighty-four pounds, and haven't eaten anything since Tuesday."

The still, small voice responded with "Finn's Deli."

I hadn't read 1 Kings 19:12. This was my first experience with the still, small voice. It's not audible, yet you "hear it" like a tune that runs through your brain even though the radio's off. It's a thought you wouldn't have arrived at on your own. It may not seem logical, either.

In the five years we'd lived in that neighborhood, I'd been to Finn's once when I was ten. I recalled that it was expensive and had a "No

Credit" sign posted over the cash register. It sat three blocks farther from our house than the stores where I usually went. Nobody in Finn's would know me. I asked a second time, and again the answer came "Finn's Deli."

Who'll iron a shirt for Mil? But the message remained clear: "Get up, get ready, and go to Finn's."

After an icy sponge bath, I borrowed another outfit from Lee's part of the closet. I gathered the clothes I'd worn the day before, along with my own two outfits, and stopped at the dry cleaner first. Tim, the owner's son, was working at the counter. He was in drama club with me.

"Could you have these clothes cleaned, pressed, and ready for me to pick up after school? Please, Tim."

"Sure, Florence. We'll send the bill to your father."

I crossed the street to Finn's and looked past the sign on the cash register that read, "Credit makes enemies. Let's be friends."

"Good morning, I'm John Calderone's daughter. May I please have a baloney sandwich on a hero roll? And would you please send the bill to my father?"

"John Calderone picks up a newspaper here every morning around eleven. Tell me the name of that paper, and I'll make you a sandwich."

"He reads an Italian one called *Il Progresso Italo-Americano.*"

Her laugh implied she'd never have expected a fair-haired, blue-eyed teen to encounter no difficulty pronouncing that title in Italian. "You'd have to live under the same roof with him to know that. Okay, I'll make your sandwich and write the charge on your father's newspaper."

I hadn't known where Pop bought *Il Progresso.* Three other stores closer to us also sold newspapers. On his night work schedule, Pop would awaken around 10:00 AM, walk to the local shops, come home, and have lunch. He slept much too soundly to try waking him early, and waking him could unleash chaos better avoided.

Neither of my parents drove cars. At 2:00 PM, Pop would catch a bus to work. He'd return home after we'd gone to sleep. But when he arrived home past midnight on that occasion, the sounds of shouting from their bedroom jolted me awake. "No, she can't eat with us, Giovanni. I have to know where she was Tuesday."

"Where does she say she was?"

"In school until 5:00 PM."

"Then she was in school."

I recalled Mom's conclusion-jumping tendencies of earlier years when she'd blamed Joe and Grace Lobo for a bad credit report. Although Pop was the one with the damaged brain, it was Mom who blocked all logical explanations.

"Don't believe her. I'm punishing her until she tells me where she really was."

"You're punishing her, but it's costing me money. I bought spiced ham and bread today. Let her make her lunch tomorrow."

"Giovanni, are you forgetting what we're dealing with? The liar who maliciously broke my lamp and the piano we spent years paying for. The one who admitted she burned down the playhouse you spent weeks building for her."

"Now, how long do I keep paying these extra bills she's running up?"

"All right. Stop hollering at me. I'll make sure she never charges anything at Finn's again."

When I got up Friday, the refrigerator once again remained devoid of food. Mom had hidden sandwiches in Mil's room for him and Lee.

Unwashed dishes continued to accumulate in the sink. The floors I had once routinely swept and vacuumed now showed several days' worth of traffic and soil. The once-gleaming dining room furniture wore a growing coat of dust.

Because Mom wouldn't leave food or money where I could find them, she'd have to buy supper groceries after work. Then, when Mom arrived home, she'd have to cook supper.

Paterson had no fast-food places where we could buy quick meals or I could find employment. Babysitting jobs didn't exist in the area. I knew of no social service agencies that helped abused teens. Adolescents who complained to school personnel, police, or priests about mistreatment at home would hear, "Teens are rebellious. Your parents love you. You must always obey them."

Running away was not an option. The streets and the gangs were no friendlier than the abusive home. Again I prayed to God. Again the same answer came. This meal would have to last me all day and possibly beyond. I went back to Finn's.

"May I have a roast beef hero with a side of coleslaw and potato salad to go, please?"

"Yes. By the way, a short lady with a heavy Italian accent—I guess it was your Mother—came in early this morning. I'm sorry, but I couldn't understand her. Do you have any idea what she wanted to tell me?"

"She didn't say anything to me today, Mrs. Finn. Sorry."

I'd get my food. Pop would get the bill when he went to buy his paper. Mom would hear about it when he got home from work around midnight. Early that evening, Mom again dispatched Lee to our room to reason with me.

"Who said you could wear my clothes?"

"Sorry, Lee. If I'd asked, you would've had to say no."

"But that's my good blouse. Mom gave it to me for my birthday."

"What's that like, Lee? I wouldn't know. I've never gotten a present from Mom or any other relative on my birthday."

She walked to the edge of our bed, sat down, and changed the subject. "Mom has decided out of the kindness of her heart to forgive you under certain conditions. First, tell her where you really were Tuesday. Second, beg her forgiveness on two bended knees. Third, promise never to lie again or to do whatever you were really doing Tuesday. Fourth, return to Mass on Sundays."

"Two bended knees? Is she nuts? That's an act of worship; I don't worship anything except God."

"I'm just relaying a message."

"You're using the words *Mom* and *kindness* in the same sentence. This has more to do with Pop's fury about the deli and the dry-cleaning bills. Mom's mad at me. Look how it snowballs." I put down the pen I'd been using for my homework and started counting on my fingers. "One: I stopped ironing Mil's shirts; now Mom gets up earlier to iron them. Two: I'm borrowing your clothes; that upsets you. Three: After her full workday, Mom does the errands and cooking I used to do. Four: Nobody washes the dishes."

She gave me that look we sometimes exchanged when our parents were arguing well into the night. It blended sympathy for our battered mom with our frustration over her stubborn refusal to reason anything logically. I could tell that Lee just wanted this problem to go away.

"Where were you really last Tuesday?"

"Lee, where would I have been that I'd have to keep so secret? Out with a boy? I go out with boys." I opened my desk drawer and retrieved the diary I knew she and my brothers had discovered, read often, quoted, and giggled over. "Remember Ernie, the swimming champ from last summer? Did you forget Bob Artus, who took me to the movies? What about Joni's friend Artie who took me bowling? Weren't they boys? Why would I have to sneak around to see a boy?" I pulled out a scrapbook that contained snapshots Joni had taken of my friends Lee had met. "For years, most weekdays I've been home alone for hours after school. If I wanted secret liaisons with anybody, I could have had them right here."

I'd have hated to be in my sister's spot. If Lee conveyed the appearance of believing me, she'd automatically become Mom's enemy. "Lee, tell Mom two things for me. First, honest, I really was at rehearsal Tuesday. Second, I'll make a counter offer of my own." I thought for a moment about this unplanned bargaining chip. "I'll cook suppers, if I'm permitted to eat a serving of what I cook. If she doesn't want me at her table, I'll eat at this desk. I'll stop charging food at the deli if I find lunch meat and bread in the refrigerator. And because I live here, I'll vacuum rugs and sweep floors on Saturdays."

Lee went back to Mom and reported that I'd agreed to make peace, but she supplied no details. Mom assumed sweet victory—unconditional surrender to all her terms. The next day, I cooked, served, and ate lunch, but Mom didn't speak to me. Afterward, with clenched lips, she awaited my confession and apologies on two bended knees. Finally, she asked Lee, "Why isn't your sister begging my forgiveness? She still hasn't started polishing the furniture or cleaning the mirrors like she's supposed to do every Saturday. Why hasn't she washed that mountain of dishes in the sink?"

"Mom, I'm not washing dishes from meals I was deemed unworthy to eat. Dishwashing was my task when everyone thought Mil shopped and Lee cooked. I agreed to prepare meals, vacuum rugs, and sweep floors. Other people live in this house, too. They can do the rest."

"But Mom expects you to return to Mass Sundays," Lee said. "You have to. One of the Ten Commandments says, 'Honor thy father and thy mother.'"

"Yeah, and the next one says, 'Thou shalt not kill,'" I said. "Anyone who tries to choke me, slash my throat, and starve me to death negates her right to blind obedience."

"Tell that slut I won't speak to her until she complies with all my terms," Mom said.

There was something liberating about not being nagged by someone who hated me too much to speak to me.

That Sunday morning while Pop and my siblings attended Mass, I learned why Mom had pressured me so hard to go. The phone rang and I answered it. A male with a thick, Neapolitan accent thought it was Mom's "hello" he'd heard.

"Hello, dear Maria. I no can wait to see you again."

"This isn't Maria. This is Florence."

"Oh. Mistake numero." He hung up, but a half hour later, he called again. Once more, after realizing Mom hadn't answered, he said he'd reached a wrong number and hung up. He called after another fifteen minutes. This time I handed the receiver to Mom. "Either this guy really keeps dialing wrong, Mom, or you're the Maria he wants to talk to."

"Hello, Mr. Sorentino,*" she said. "Yes, I can work overtime for you Saturday. You're such a kind boss. See you tomorrow."

For years Mom had said that her boss was a Jewish man named Frank Saltz. In subsequent conversations I'd overhear, she'd tell Lee that Mr. Sorentino was as a fabric cutter and a garment presser at the factory.

I didn't reveal her little secret. It would have made major trouble. I had no idea how innocent or sordid this friendship or work relationship was.

Part 4

STILL-DEFIANT YOUNG ADULT

Chapter 18

LATER TEENS

A FEW MONTHS after the knife incident, Mom just barely started speaking to me, but kept her distance. I guess she took her own often-quoted advice "Be nice to anyone who's in a position to hurt you." Those Sunday morning phone calls continued. They could have been more innocent than they seemed. Still, if I were to tell Pop about them, the death-before-dishonor mentality would take over. Even if it meant the electric chair, Pop would avenge his honor by murdering them both.

By then I had buried my memories of the past and thought that Mom had also. I still wasn't attending any church or getting any closer to knowing God. I recalled what I considered an accurate ingredient of the catechism: "God is omniscient, omnipotent, and omnipresent." He made that evident in all he'd brought me through. At home, the only complete Bible was the one Mom had received in the hospital when her appendix had burst. I could read Italian, but Mom kept the precious book locked away.

As for my future plans, I still hoped to become a high school teacher. This required three specialties on a teaching license. I'd major in English, Italian, and Art. Paterson State Teachers College occupied a former grade school building four blocks from our house.

"Because of an acute teacher shortage," my guidance counselor said, "tuition is only fifty dollars per semester. For a total of $400 plus the cost of textbooks, you could receive a four-year teaching degree. Start saving and go after it."

At sixteen, I found part-time work in a photo studio. I opened a savings account at County Bank with twenty-five dollars toward tuition and books. I intended to pay for college from my earnings. I figured I'd live at home to save on commuting but continue working part-time and pay half my wages to Mom in board money. One evening I told Mom my plans.

"So that's the bad news you have prepared for me? I should have made you quit school and start factory work the day you legally could—on your sixteenth birthday."

"Bad news? Mom, you've always bragged to me about your friends' daughters who became teachers. I thought you'd be proud to have a daughter teaching school."

"You don't deserve it. College for you would be a waste of four years. We educate our sons because they'll support families someday."

For a while I put my college plans on hold. I continued to give Mom half my part-time earnings but needed the rest for lunch and commuting costs. I also had to cover graduation expenses—cap and gown, yearbook, class ring, and prom gown. Yes, much to Mom's amazement, I received *three* invitations to my prom. The first one, which I accepted, came from a college sophomore I'd met two years earlier.

One Saturday afternoon about a month before my graduation, a new family in town surprised us with a visit. Toto introduced his third wife, a red-haired Texan named Ginger, and her three children. The teenaged boy addressed Mom as "Ma'am," typical of the young, southern gentleman he'd learned to be. His preteen sister's vocabulary appeared limited to a stoic "Hello." A five-year-old named Jenny came bounding in with hugs and smiles to command the spotlight.

"Your brother Toto sure is spoilin' our little Jenny," Ginger told Mom. "He takes her bye-bye with him, snaps photos of her, buys her presents. She just loves bein' his precious princess."

I eyed the little blonde in the pink pinafore, and my heart could have burst. I longed to pick her up and scream, "Don't! Don't trust that monster; don't let him near her." But sometimes we'll go through life regretting that we didn't say something, so we don't go through life regretting that we did.

"Maria, can I have a word with you in private?" Toto said.

Mom and Toto disappeared into the kitchen for a few minutes. This time she emerged without the usual beige envelope, she seemed to have all the other times he'd asked to see her alone.

The next time we heard from him several months had gone by. The official word Ginger issued to the family was "For the sake of the children, I've sued Toto for divorce."

I started going to Saturday square dances with Jay,* a young man I'd met where I worked. Despite what Mom said about me, guys like Jay treated me with respect. One evening as we discussed religion, he pulled a red New Testament out of his pocket and handed it to me. Knowing Mom would confiscate it, I stashed it in the back of my messy homework desk drawer.

Occasionally, my personal cheering section and official shoulder to cry on, Eddie Fitzmaurice, stopped by. "I just picked up this new car, Florence. Want to test-drive it?"

"You trust me to drive your new Caddy convertible?"

"Yup. My girl, Sandra*, doesn't get to, though."

"Why me and not her?"

"She refuses to go anywhere with me in my old Ford heap. You never care what junk I show up in. You don't just like me for my cars; you like me for myself."

"And you think Sandra just likes you for your classy car?"

"Yup."

Although Eddie would have many other girlfriends, I wondered why any guy would date a girl he thought was that shallow. There was never a romance between us. I just enjoyed his humor, personality, and great company.

In the final three weeks before diplomas, almost every high school senior said it. "I'm not going to graduate." In my case, had it not been for Miss Monks, that would have been a certainty. She'd been my English teacher the previous year. Now I would breeze past her classroom door between fourth and fifth periods. In all my other classes, I'd been running a straight A average. But in my final semester of high school, I had to pass typing to graduate.

Most teenagers in Paterson didn't own typewriters then. We needed to complete one long, grueling error-free assignment per day on a manual Underwood in class. A final requirement was the sustained speed test—forty words per minute for ten non stop minutes with fewer than five errors.

As that semester started, typing teacher Mrs. Dobbs was out on extended medical leave. Her substitute received our completed daily work in the upper tier of a two-tier box on her desk.

"You're right on schedule with assignments," the sub told me, "but a tad shy of the forty-word-per-minute mark. You'll make it soon."

"I'm almost there. Last speed test I typed thirty-nine."

That school year I was out sick just one day, the day Mrs. Dobbs returned to announce a major change. "Hand all your completed typing assignments in by placing them into the lower tier of the box on my desk. The upper tier is where I put papers I've finished grading. They're there for the janitor to discard."

Next day, I asked several classmates, "Did anything happen yesterday I should know about?"

"Nope. Mrs. Dobbs came back; that's about it."

In ignorance, I continued handing in my finished class work to the upper tier, now the "out box." Weeks later came "warning day," when students received notification of impending doom on their report cards. "You're failing typing," Mrs. Dobbs told me. "You've yet to turn in any assignments since I got back."

In the unpleasant exchange that followed, I learned about the "in-box" switch. How easy it would have been for her to label the boxes "In" and "Out" with the little tags that designated each box's purpose.

"We have fifteen school days left, Mrs. Dobbs. I'm now missing twenty days' worth of work. If I came in last period every day, I could retype fifteen of the twenty. Would that be acceptable?"

"Absolutely not. I want all the missing assignments in fifteen days, or you don't graduate."

"Mrs. Dobbs, fifteen out of twenty would be 75 percent. Seventy is a passing grade in our school."

She wouldn't budge. Next morning, the teachers' lounge was abuzz about my rotten Sicilian temper and disrespect for Mrs. Dobbs. The rest of the faculty either scolded or shunned me.

I talked to God about it. "You know if I don't graduate on the first try, it won't ever happen. Mom won't stand for my going to summer school or another semester of high school."

It seemed as though God whispered, "Watch me." Thursday morning Miss Monks intercepted me in the corridor and yanked me into her classroom. "This isn't like you, Florence. What's going on?"

Through my sobs, I blurted out my side of the ugly tale. Friday, she stopped me in the halls to hand me a green metal container with a carrying handle on top.

"I got this portable typewriter as my own high school graduation gift. Take it home. Catch up on your assignments. Then return it."

That weekend I told my family, "If the phone or doorbell should ring for me, please take a message. I'm not available."

Monday morning my former English teacher frowned when I set the heavy, green container back on her desk. "Did you give up already, Florence? Aren't you going to even try and complete the backlog?"

"It's all done Miss Monks, and thank you. Typing for ten solid hours on Saturday and ten on Sunday brought my speed up to fifty-three words per minute." I felt like the gold medalist at the Olympics. "I'm graduating on time."

She imparted so much more than conjugations, figures of speech, and poetic meters. Miss Monks personified the intent of the Golden Rule.

Because my graduation came two months before my sister Lee's wedding, Mom warned me not to expect the celebrations or gifts my older brothers had received. When my godmother, Grace Lobo, asked Mom what she was buying me for graduation, Mom said she'd bought a portable typewriter.

"Next time we come over, my daughter, Millie, will want to see it. She's also learning how to type."

"I haven't picked it up yet, Comare Grace; it's on layaway."

Now Mom stood to lose face and felt cornered into showing something to back up her lie.

"When we're downtown, pick out a portable typewriter," she said that evening. "God knows I can't afford it, and you don't deserve it, but we'll have to. Your godmother thinks I bought you one."

I selected an Underwood manual that bore a modest price tag of $50. Mom put $5 down on it and signed an agreement to pay it off in installments of $5 per week. When the first payment fell due, she said, "Stop by the store on your way to your after-school job and make this week's installment on the typewriter. I'll pay you back later."

I took $5 that I had allocated toward lunch and carfare and made the payment. This continued each week until I had paid the entire $50 plus interest. She never reimbursed me. I attributed this mistake to an oversight triggered by her preoccupation with Lee's wedding plans and didn't mention it again.

One day she came home raving about a beautiful winter coat she wanted me to have. "Grace bought one like it for Millie. Why should Grace outdo me?"

"Mom, Millie's an only child. She's always had lots of things I could never have."

"Come to the store and look at the coat. I guarantee you'll want one for yourself."

We rode the bus to the clothing boutique in Passaic that displayed the fake fur in its window. One glance and I hated it. The price was more than twice what my "graduation present" had cost. To make Mom happy, we went inside where a salesperson brought us the coat for a closer look. The label said it had to be dry-cleaned by the costlier-than-normal "fur coat method." Its eggshell-white color would require cleanings after almost every wearing, making it much too expensive to maintain. I disliked the style. Almost ankle length, it featured dolman sleeves and a flared back. When I tried it on, I resembled an overweight polar bear about to deliver twin cubs.

"Mom, on a sixty-one-inch-tall person like me, this coat would look like a mass of fur walking down the street. Besides, it's much more than I can afford to buy or to have dry-cleaned. And it's so dressy. I'd rarely, if ever, have occasion to wear something like this."

"You have no taste. Don't you know elegance when you see it?"

How would I have gained a taste for elegance? Never having had the chance to buy clothes, I'd grown up waiting for Lee to outgrow her castoffs.

Mom fumed as we left the store. She was used to wielding control over Lee's thoughts—getting her to agree she loved everything Mom liked and abhorred everything Mom despised. I expressed my true opinions. Mom loathed that trait in me. The following workday, she came home with the coat and handed it to me. "I bought it for you. It's a gift."

I thanked her, but still with no occasion that called for this formal a garment, I hung it in the closet. Thirty days later, a man identifying himself as the store's credit manager phoned. "Is this Florence Calderone? The balance on your account with us is four weeks in arrears. You haven't made one payment since you put $3 down on the white Borgana coat you purchased." He began a long diatribe threatening to involve collection agencies, lawsuits, and my credit rating.

"I didn't purchase the coat; my mother did."

"You signed a contract agreeing to make weekly installment payments of $10 plus interest."

"I didn't sign anything. My mother brought the coat home and told me it was a gift."

"I remember this transaction, miss. The customer was about fifty and spoke with a thick Italian accent."

"Do I sound like her to you? Look, I'm seventeen years old. If there's a signature on your paperwork, it isn't mine. Even if it were, as a minor I could legally rescind the contract. You're welcome to refund the $3 down-payment and repossess the unused coat."

Furious with me for refusing to knuckle under and pay for her purchase, Mom hurled a barrage of ugly names at me. She eventually settled with the store and wound up owning the coat.

One Saturday morning on her way to "work overtime," she strode out of the house in it like a Paris runway model. By 6:00 PM the hem, cuffs, and pockets looked as though she'd been shoveling coal, then wiping sweaty hands on them. Before long, she realized how much better it had looked on a six-foot mannequin and how impractical the purchase had been.

Chapter 19

TRUST

FOLLOWING GRADUATION, I found full-time work as a secretary in Manhattan at a salary of sixty dollars per week. The commercial weekly rate for room and board was five dollars, but before the postwar building boom, housing remained scarce. I told Mom I'd give her twenty dollars each week and bank another twenty toward college night school classes. The rest would go toward income taxes, lunch, clothing, and train fare.

"I stop at County Bank to cash my paycheck every Friday after work," Mom said. "Give me your passbook, and while I'm there I'll make your deposits for you."

The following Friday morning, she pulled a dozen deposit slips from her tan, plastic purse and handed them to me. I located my navy-blue bankbook and watched her drop it into that same handbag. From that point, each week I'd give her a twenty in board money and another twenty with a completed deposit slip.

"Thanks for saving me the trip to the bank, Mom."

"It's not out of my way. See, I'm tucking the deposit slip and this other twenty into your savings passbook. I'll deposit it into your account later today."

During my commute, I rode subways and began reading the posters placed there by the New York Bible Society. The verses ran for a month, each beginning with "Jesus said." One was "Labour not for the meat which perisheth, but for that meat which endureth unto everlasting life" (John 6:27 KJV). The following month's was "Come unto me, all ye that labour and are heavy laden, and I will give you rest" (Matt. 11:28 KJV). Then, "Search the scriptures, for in them ye think ye have eternal life: and they are they which testify of me" (John 5:39).

I went home, dug out that red book my square dance partner, Jay, had given me and started reading. Since Lee had married and I had the bedroom all to myself, it was easier to hide things.

One day a young woman I'd met at work asked if I'd share an apartment in New York City with her. "You could save on train fare and live close to work in a friendly household."

I seriously considered her offer. Then God intervened. I found out my would-be roommate had become pregnant by her married lover, a frequent visitor to the apartment. No, I didn't need to be part of a household that was that "friendly."

And God had known what would happen next. Six months after I started my secretarial job, my boss called me into his office. "Our accountant says we're forced to reduce expenses, so I'm cutting our last two staff positions here. Please find other employment; you've earned an excellent reference here."

The want ad in the *Paterson Evening News* read, "Two Bank Tellers. HS grad. Min. six months' office exp. and good reference. Apply in person. First Federal Savings."

I went to work for First Federal Savings. The other new hire was a devout evangelical named Lillian. The bank put me in charge of processing incoming mail transactions, including "demand drafts." These official request forms required no passbooks, but through customers' signatures authorized transfers between banks. Since First Federal paid 4 percent interest while County Bank paid 1 percent, I opened a savings account where I worked.

I still gave Mom twenty dollars per week, which covered the eighty-dollar monthly mortgage payment on the house. I still paid for my own food, clothing, and bus fare.

On my first payday at the bank, I gave Mom her usual twenty in board money. "Where's the other twenty for me to put in County Bank for you?"

"Mom, I opened an account at First Federal. They pay four times the interest."

"You'll be tempted to spend it if it's right at your elbow. I'll take it and deposit it for you."

"I already deposited it into my college fund at work, Mom. Could I please have my other passbook so I can merge the two accounts at the higher interest rate?"

"It's in my other purse upstairs. I'll get it later."

Anytime I mentioned the passbook, she'd stall. The next payday I sent County Bank a demand draft: "Balance of account plus interest to First Federal." Four business days later, at work I greeted the arrival of my college fund's transfer. Since I'd given Mom $20 extra per week for the six months I'd worked in New York, I expected the check to total over $520. This would have covered several semesters of night classes at the time. At first, I thought I'd misread it: "Twenty-six dollars and seventeen cents." Certain they'd made an error, I phoned County Bank.

"This is Florence Calderone. My mother deposited twenty dollars into my savings account every Friday for the past six months. Can you tell me what account those deposits were credited to?"

For a few minutes, I heard papers rustling. "Miss Calderone, no deposits have been made to any account here for you in the last three years. Your only account with us was inactive until we transferred it to First Federal yesterday."

"May I speak to the manager, please?"

"You're talking to the manager. I know Mrs. Calderone. Short lady, black wavy hair, thick Italian accent. She's here every Friday at 5:30 but never makes deposits to anything with your name on it."

"And this is the County Bank on 21st Avenue next to Kaznica's Drug Store?"

"That's correct."

That evening, I got home ten minutes before Mom and began cooking. When Mom walked in after work, I thought we'd clarify the financial mystery.

"Mom, into which bank book did you deposit my college savings?"

"You know, the navy-blue book. It's County Bank by my bus stop. Why?"

"May I see that passbook please, Mom?"

She groaned and draped her coat over the dining room chair.

"I'm tired now. Give me a chance to sit down. I keep your book in my other purse."

"You showed me you were putting it in the tan purse you're holding now."

"Why do you keep bringing up that silly bank book? Don't you trust me?"

"I don't trust the bank. I transferred the account, and they said it had about twenty-six dollars in it. I want to take the actual record of deposits and show them their mistake."

A scowl crossed her face. It resembled the venomous look that preceded most of her conversations with my father. "You're a rotten liar. Everybody knows you can't withdraw money from a bank without a passbook."

"It's done by demand draft, Mom. I do them for customers at work every day."

Now out of arguments, she opened her purse, took out the blue booklet, and slammed it onto the dining room table. Except for the original twenty-five-dollar entry notated years earlier, every page was blank. I looked at the woman who'd often pummeled me to underscore how contemptible lying was.

"Mom, what happened to the money you claimed to be banking for me?"

"You think I get rich with that miserable twenty-dollar pittance you give me? You owe me every cent you ever get." She hurled the purse on the dining room floor, spilling keys, coins, and lipstick. "What about when you broke my lamp and the piano or when you burned down the playhouse? You still owe me for those. Remember when you claimed to be in school, but nobody was there to answer the phone?"

I walked into the kitchen to stir the stew I'd started cooking earlier. This would be another memorable supper.

"You don't deserve to be my daughter or to live here, you ugly slut. You should be begging me to forgive you."

I wondered how long the sham would have continued. But I still left the "miserable pittance" of half my net pay where I knew she'd find it each week. Although she'd slam doors and drawers and grumble whenever I entered a room, I again enjoyed the eerie freedom of not being nagged. I knew the silent treatment wouldn't last as long as I kept fielding phone calls from Mr. Sorentino each Sunday. As I pondered that picture, some facets explained themselves. If Pop thought Mom was at work most Saturdays, he'd expect her to have overtime pay to show for it. How convenient of me to supply her with all those weeks' worth of credibility.

Except for the borgana coat incident, Mom had never been attentive to her wardrobe. One day she came home with a stylish, slate-gray, linen outfit she handed me. "I bought this for you."

At ninety-four pounds, I wore what is today size-eight petite, the smallest clothing then available from Paterson retailers. Even these garments were too roomy for me. If Lee's clothes came close to fitting me, it was because she also had a twenty-inch waistline at the time. But at 145 pounds, Mom wore a women's size fourteen. I tried on the outfit. The sleeves were several inches wider than my shoulders and drooped down my arms like deflated balloons. The skirt wouldn't stay up around my waist and dropped to the floor.

"Mom, this is awfully nice of you, but it's a size fourteen. That's way too big on me. Can you exchange it for a smaller size?"

"You miserable ingrate! No, I can't exchange it. It was on sale, and that was the smallest size they had." She exhaled her official martyred-mother sigh and picked up the garment. "If you won't wear it, I guess I'll have to."

Two weeks later, the same thing happened involving a black velvet, dressy suit she bought and a stunning pair of high-heeled shoes. In each case, the item happened to be much too big for me but exactly her size. Each time, by default, she wound up with a fancy new garment for herself.

"Where are you getting all these new clothes all of a sudden?" Pop said.

"I buy them for Florence. I want her to dress elegantly now so she can attract a potential husband. But there's no pleasing her; she rejects everything I bring home. So rather than waste the money, I'm forced to use them myself."

When she'd "work" on Saturdays, instead of her usual threadbare dresses, she'd wear one of the lovely outfits and shoes she'd "intended for me." One Saturday afternoon, she returned with a dark; red stain on the bodice of her velvet frock. "Our boss, Mr. Sorentino, took us all out to lunch. He drove us in his car to an Italian restaurant, and I spilled marinara sauce on me."

I had once overheard Mom tell Lee that this man drove the cutest little Fiat Toppolino. No bigger than a Volkswagen Beetle, this would hardly accommodate a fraction of the workers in Mom's department. On another Saturday, she came home sporting a one-carat diamond ring.

Let me guess what the official explanation will be this time, Mom. Mr. Sorentino bought bonus gifts for your whole department. Or you bought it for me; it'll be way too big but will fit you perfectly.

Pop spotted it above her thin, gold wedding band. "Where did that diamond ring come from?"

"I won it in a raffle. The Red Cross was holding a fund-raiser at a restaurant our boss drove us to on our lunch hour. We all bought tickets. Mine won."

"This family does well with raffles, doesn't it?" Pop said. "Jerry won the TV set a few years ago; now you won this nice diamond ring."

Mom shot a troubled-afterthought glance at me. "Oh, if you happen to talk to Comare Grace's daughter, Millie, or any of my coworkers, don't tell them about this. People get envious if they know someone else won something."

How strange. If all her coworkers were there when the drawing was held, wouldn't they have noticed whose ticket won? Also strange—how this "lottery prize" just happened to be exactly the right size for the winner's finger.

An acquaintance alerted me to the availability of an apartment for rent. I again looked into the possibility of living on my own, but again God intervened. In its kitchen a lingering odor of garlic sauce mixed with stale cigar smoke. I could have gotten past that, but as the landlord showed me the flat, he acted much too affectionate.

"I live right downstairs, darling. If you ever need me for anything, anytime day or night, you call me, understand? I'll be right over."

"How much is the rent?"

"For you, sweetheart, $50 a month."

"Does that include utilities?"

He squeezed my upper arm. "Well, no, but if you haven't got it, honey, I'm sure we can work something out."

Maybe my mother was right. Sometimes there is no pleasing me. This time, for instance, a perfectly good, inexpensive apartment became available. Its rent for a month was about what I netted in a week. Yet I bypassed the chance to take it.

Chapter 2o ❧

THREE DATES, SAME PARTY

SOMETIMES JERRY OR Mil, now in the Navy, would come home on weekends with shipmates. "Your brother can't stop bragging about you," they'd tell me. "He really misses you and loves you a lot."

Really? Weren't these the same brothers who couldn't torment me enough when we were kids? I guess they were maturing.

When it came to dating, Mom had imposed her unbendable rule on me. "Any guy you date must first come to the house and meet me. He won't get improper ideas about you if he knows your mother can pick him out of a lineup."

The summer after I turned nineteen, my social life plunged into a deep slump. I seemed destined to warm a bench in the dugout of dating's minor leagues.

Joni had moved to another part of town and seldom called now. Many of my female friends became engaged to guys they met through their jobs or colleges. Most of my male friends either had moved to university dorms or were doing military service. The telephone hadn't rung for me in so long that I checked periodically to make sure it still worked.

One evening it finally rang. "Hi, Flo," former high school classmate Paul said. "We're having an Alumni Talent Revue next month. Want to be in some comedy skits?"

"Sounds good, Paul. Thanks for asking."

"Rehearsals start Monday at 7:00 PM in the school auditorium."

"Great. Count me in."

I rode a bus to the first practice session, where I reconnected with old friends and met new cast members. One of the alumni I remet was magician "Baffling Bob." A five-six platinum blond with cherubic features and gold-rimmed glasses, he donned a black tux for his magic act. When we discovered we lived two blocks apart, he offered to drive me to future rehearsals.

Sandy-haired trombonist, Johnny, stood five feet eleven and had angular features and dark-rimmed glasses. He sported bright red, prep school, brass-buttoned blazers. We'd met before. Two years earlier, Johnny had asked me to my senior prom on such short notice, I'd already accepted another invitation.

Newly arrived from North Carolina, bluegrass musicians Roy and Donald spoke with southern drawls and wore light-gray cowboy outfits. Roy's curly, flame-red hair topped his six-six frame that was increased by two-inch high heels on his cowboy boots. His jet-black-haired brother, Donald stood six feet two.

Four weeks later, following the show, our director announced, "Come to the cast party, everybody. It's Friday at 7:00 PM in the school cafeteria."

"Flo, I'll drive you to the party Friday," Baffling Bob said.

"Sorry, Bob. I can't go. I have to be at a close friend's bridal shower Friday."

Later, trombonist Johnny came by. "Hey, Flo, why don't I take you to the cast party?"

"Wish I could go to it, Johnny, but I already planned to attend a bridal shower that night."

"You realize this is the second time I've asked you for a date and the second time you've turned me down. Should I take a hint?"

"No, really, Johnny, I'd love to go with you, but honest, I made these other plans weeks ago."

Within minutes bluegrass singer Roy stopped me. "I'd sure like it if you could be my date to that cast party"

"Oh, how sweet. Thanks so much Roy, but I can't. A dear friend is getting married, and I agreed to go to her bridal shower that day."

As I mingled, gathering autographs on my souvenir program, prop-manager Joey stepped up. "Flo, is there any way you can skip that dumb bridal shower?"

How I longed to say I could! I hated turning down three dates after the social desert I'd been in for months. The cast party sounded like so much more fun than a boring old-hen party. The shower would require taking two buses in each direction to a strange neighborhood after dark. "I suppose l could just send a gift . . ."

"Yippee!" Joey yelled, "Flo's going to the cast party."

In those days most dating was innocent enough, and playing the field was honorable for respectable girls. But there was still the problem of three individuals assuming I'd be going as their date. I decided if anyone mentioned picking me up for the party, I'd say I'd go stag and request a rain check. But nobody broached the subject again. Now I figured all three guys had accepted my original refusal as final and had determined to go without me. I also thought that Bob was the only one who knew where I lived.

Friday, I took the bus to the party. Then Baffling Bob walked in. "I drove to your house, but your mom said you left already. Can I get you something to eat?"

My first thought was to find a tactful way to explain the "three-invitation-I'm-really-here-stag mix-up." But as I started to decline food, I spotted Johnny arriving.

"Thanks, Bob," I said. "Please get me a sandwich."

Bob went to the long buffet line.

"I got your address from another cast member. I found your house and stopped there first," Johnny said. "Your mother told me you'd left already."

Just then, Marilyn walked up and interrupted with "Johnny, when are you going to return my record player and all those albums you borrowed?"

"Can't that wait?" Johnny said. "I've wanted to date this girl for two years. Now that I finally got her to go out with me, I'm not going to walk away from her."

"But I need that stuff for my birthday tomorrow."

"Johnny, why don't you and Marilyn go get her record player and albums right now?" I said. "You don't want to spoil her birthday."

"Gosh, Flo, you sure you don't mind? I'd take you with us, but the equipment I borrowed won't fit in the car with three people. Be right back."

Just as Bob returned with my sandwich, Roy's brother, Donald, arrived.

"Bob, could you get me a soda please?" I said. Bob then got into the beverage line.

"Roy's been delayed," Donald said. "His buddy from North Carolina showed up unexpectedly. I tried to find you at your house, but by the time I did, your mom said you'd left already."

"Donald, please tell Roy he should be with his buddy tonight. The guy drove all this distance to see him."

"Really? Thanks, you're awfully understanding about this." He dashed out. But when Bob returned with my cola, I spotted Roy himself entering.

Think, Florence. He got you food; he got you a soda. What else will keep Bob busy for a while? "Bob, why don't you do some magic tricks for us?"

The magician took out a deck of cards, and a fascinated audience crowded around him. He couldn't hear Roy say, "Flo, I was just at your house . . ."

". . . and my mom said I left already. Roy, I told your brother you shouldn't be with me tonight. You should be entertaining that friend from North Carolina."

"No, Flo. When I make a date, I keep it."

"Roy, I insist. I can always take a rain check, but how often do you get to see your hometown buddy?"

"Flo, you're . . ."

"Yeah, I know. I'm the most understanding girl you ever met."

After Roy departed, prop manager Joey shouted an announcement. "Listen, everybody. The custodians need to lock this building so they don't run into overtime. This party's moving to Allen's house. Follow me."

Bob drove me to Allen's, where the TV set aired the world champion-ship wrestling matches. Engrossed in the contests, he didn't notice when Johnny returned to bombard me with apologies. "I've been searching all over for this relocated party. Now that I finally made it, the evening is shot. Let me drive you home and plead for a rain check."

I glanced at Bob, who remained mesmerized by a cathode ray tube. Over the din, I said, "Bob, I have an early day tomorrow, so I should head out. Please stay and enjoy the matches. Mind if I catch another ride home?"

He looked up. "Oh, thanks, Flo. You're awfully nice about this."

Now I wondered how my tough, uncompromising mother would react to my four gentlemen callers.

"Did that guy ever find you?" she asked when I walked in.

"What guy, Mom?"

"A boy's been here asking for you since right after you went out. I kept telling him you'd left already, but he kept coming back."

"Yeah, Mom, he found me. He just drove me home." So much for her unbendable rule.

Did I ever get to redeem any of those rain checks? Considering how this fiasco started out, I'd deem a ratio of two out of three pretty good. "Baffling Bob" returned to his junior year at college and eventually became an MD. Although he was pleasant, thoughtful, and friendly, we never became romantic. It didn't surprise me that I didn't hear from him again.

To make up for "having left me stranded" when his buddy from North Carolina arrived, Roy later took me to a movie. Our height disparity made me uncomfortable enough to wonder why he'd want to date me. Roy eventually married a woman who at six feet tall stood much closer to his towering height.

I landed back in the major leagues of dating again. Johnny continued to call frequently and took me out several months after the cast party. Lots of other girls, including my Comare Grace's daughter, Millie, liked him and envied me. But Johnny and I didn't get serious; God had other plans for me.

Chapter 21

LILLIAN

MEANWHILE AT THE bank, I'd open mail sent in by an evangelical Christian man who enclosed a gospel tract with his mortgage payments. Most of my coworkers laughed at him, but I looked forward to the salvation messages. Coworker Lillian quoted Scriptures frequently. One day I asked what religion she was.

"I was saved when I was twenty-six," she said.

"What do you mean when you say you were 'saved'?"

"I accepted Jesus as my Savior."

I had remembered hearing that expression when I attended Mrs. Bulmer's Bible class at the age of ten. Back then, I didn't understand the definition of "Savior." I thought that if you didn't reject Jesus, you had accepted him.

I had many more questions than Lillian could answer. A few weeks later, she invited me to an old-fashioned gospel revival at her church. I bought my first complete English Bible to take with me.

After I went to the revival, I started attending another church about a mile from home Sunday mornings and evenings. Yet again, I'd reunite with the congregation the care givers from my infancy had attended. Former Bible class teacher, Mrs. Bulmer, still lived a few blocks from us. Her family took me to the first service and helped introduce me. Mom told my sister she hated my beliefs. But she seemed relieved to get me out of the house. She'd again be home alone for her secret phone calls.

I signed up for evening college classes, but after my first semester, Mom broke another long stretch of the punitive silent treatment. She showed me a past-due power bill. "If you don't give me the money to pay this, they're going to cut our electricity off."

I couldn't understand it. With all three household members employed and the other duplex apartment's rent coming in, why were we always broke? Although I'd continued my steadfast board payments that covered the mortgage, I gave Mom the savings I had earmarked for my next semester's tuition. Thereafter, she continued to find ways and reasons to appropriate any funds I'd planned to use for schooling.

One Sunday afternoon, Mil's pal Ken stopped by to invite me to the movies. We'd been friends since I was thirteen. Whenever he found himself dateless, he'd think of me. Sometimes Ken, my brothers, my girlfriends, and I would go somewhere as a group. Because of his close friendship with Mil and Jerry, it seemed more like being out with another brother than with a date.

"Sorry, Ken, I'm going to church tonight."

"What? You're going to church twice on the same day? Flo, you're becoming a fanatic."

Ken stopped by the next day, handed me a slip of paper with a phone number on it, and grinned. "This is your type of message."

I phoned it, and heard a monotone voice reading, "We have a message for you from the Bible. Jesus said, "I am the way, the truth, and the life . . .""

Curious to know whether it was a recording or a live person, I interrupted with "Okay, but how can I prove it?"

She stopped reading. "Don't try to prove it. Just take it as a little child."

Yes, that's what had been missing—what I needed to accept. It matched Christ's words in Luke 18:17 (KJV). "Whosoever shall not receive the kingdom of God as a little child shall in no wise enter therein."

A few months after I'd started attending church, the woman in charge of Sunday school asked me to teach a class.

"Me, teach Sunday school? I've never even been to Sunday school."

I expected her to laugh and agree with me that the idea was absurd. She didn't.

"You learn by teaching. Come to our teacher training classes Tuesdays at 6:00 PM."

I started taking the classes taught by a Child Evangelism missionary and began teaching twelve boys aged nine to eleven. They were bussed in from the rough neighborhoods that surrounded downtown. Messy and unruly, these precious, rough-and-tumble street kids were my kind of people.

For the first time, I heard some well-known Bible stories, such as the Passover. Still too immature in my faith, I didn't know the connection between the blood of the Passover Lamb and the Messiah. I had, and still have, much more to learn. But God is patient.

Chapter 22

MAMA'S ILLNESS

AT THE SUPPER table one evening, Mom sighed, frowned, and shifted in her chair.

"What's the matter, Mom?"

She patted a spot just above her collarbone. I couldn't see it beneath her dress collar. "When I was getting dressed, I found something that feels like an almond under the skin here. It's probably nothing."

"A strange lump should be checked by a doctor, Mom. Let me get you an appointment right away."

"No, you know how I feel about doctors. They tell you to take two aspirins and then charge you a week's pay."

"But lumps could be benign or malignant. It's best to catch them early . . ."

"It doesn't hurt or anything."

Weeks later, I asked about the lump again. It had grown to the size of an eggplant. I gasped and then dashed straight to the phone to call our nearest physician. Because we still didn't have a car, we'd have to walk the four blocks to his office. I grabbed her wrist and pulled her out the door like a harbor tugboat escorting a cruiser.

"Leave me alone. I told you I don't want a doctor. Now I'm sorry I ever mentioned it."

"Don't worry about the expense, Mom. You have Blue Cross insurance through your union."

Our local general practitioner referred her to an oncologist, who performed a biopsy. The lab reported serious widespread malignancy. Back then, they didn't tell a patient when it was cancer because in advanced stages the disease was usually fatal. "This has spread so far that we don't even know where the primary site was," the specialist said. "I think she'll be gone in a month. I'm going to give her heavy doses of painkillers."

Mom lingered for several more months. Now I was the only one of her children left at home. The older ones had married and started families in other states. Mom's brothers, who visited occasionally, were a divided camp. Half said, "You're a bad daughter unless you quit your job to stay at home and care for your mother full-time." The other half said, "You're a bad daughter if you don't take a second job and hire a full-time nurse for her." Pop wanted me to continue exactly as I was; my entire salary now paid for her prescriptions. Her limited group Blue Cross coverage paid the doctor bills.

I'd get up mornings, boil syringes and needles for twenty minutes, and administer her pain shots. The midday shots were handled by a visiting public health nurse. After work, I had to give pain shots every two hours throughout the night, boiling syringes twenty minutes each time. I also had to prepare all meals, spoon-feed Mom, bathe, and groom her. Between those tasks, I cleaned house and washed bed linens. One afternoon while I shampooed her hair, she asked, "Why are you doing this?"

"Because it needs to be done, Mom."

"But I never imagined that *you* would take care of me if I got sick."

"Did you think I could just let you suffer in pain and ignore your needs?"

"I know I was never a good mother to you."

I guess that was as close to verbalizing an apology as she could manage.

Seven months later, I dashed out to the drugstore to refill her Demerol prescription. On the walk back, I bumped into an old friend. "This is

Esther," he said of the tall silver-haired woman next to him. "She's a dynamic volunteer with Billy Graham's 1957 New York Crusade."

"Would you like to go to the crusade?" Esther said as she shook my hand. "Tickets are scarce, but I have three left for Thursday's meeting."

"I'd love to go, but since my mother is confined to bed with terminal cancer, I have to stay close to home to take care of her."

"I want to meet your mother. When may I come over?"

Next evening she rang our doorbell. I led her to Mama's bedside and introduced them. "Hello, Maria," she said. "Will you come to the Billy Graham Crusade tomorrow? The bus leaves from my church at 6:00 PM. I will drive you to the bus stop."

"Yes, I'll go," Mama whispered. That shocked me. Mama, who refused to attend church, hadn't been out of bed in weeks for any reason. Her lingering illness now required pain-numbing injections every two hours. How could she manage a ninety-minute bus ride, plus hours at the crusade? Couldn't Esther tell that Mama was on her deathbed? But why argue with God's perfect plans?

She was fifty-six when we received the horrible news of her terminal illness.

On the blessed day Esther took us to the crusade, Dr. Graham began with "The Bible says, 'It is appointed unto men once to die, but after this the judgment'" (Heb. 9:27 KJV).

This message went straight to Mom's heart. Although nobody told her she had cancer, Mom suspected that she'd be gone soon. At Graham's invitation, Esther took Mom's arm and said, "Would you like to go forward and give your life to Christ?"

"Oh, yes," Mom said.

It took hours to get her ready to come here tonight, I thought. *Mama can't even walk twelve feet from the bed to the bathroom. How will she ever cover the distance from the top tier of Madison Square Garden's Felt Forum across the vast auditorium to the front platform?*

As the crusade choir began singing "Just As I Am," Mom leaned one arm on Esther's shoulder and one on mine. We took baby steps to the podium's base. At first I wondered whether she really understood what she was doing. *Can she be going through these heroic motions just to impress Esther?* But was I wrong! What a change God made in Mom.

When she got to the "terminal" stage, she was admitted to the local Catholic hospital. I rode the bus there on my lunch hours and after work. For the first time, Mama smiled when she saw me arrive, and she spoke kind words to me. Despite her language barrier, before hospital staff and visitors, she'd praise and glorify Christ.

She wouldn't eat anything unless I fed it to her. Fearing she'd be too much trouble to the hospital staff, she suspected they'd poison her food to get rid of her. She refused to let anyone but me wash her hair or teeth. During my daily visits, she'd ask me to read to her from her Italian Bible.

One day she brought up a subject I didn't expect: "Next time Mr. Sorentino calls, please tell him to visit me here. I have something important to tell him."

The following Monday, she said, "Did you give Mr. Sorentino my message? What did he say?"

"He hasn't called since you entered the hospital, Mom, at least not when I've been home."

"I guess he doesn't want the surprising bit of news I have to tell him."

Soon Mom began lapsing in and out of comas. The medical facility's head nun called me aside. "We want the hospital chaplain, Father Murray, to give your mother the sacrament of extreme unction."

"You mean the last rites."

"Yes, so she has a better chance of going to heaven when she dies."

"Sister Catherine, she doesn't need a man to mumble something in Latin over her to get into heaven. Christ died for her so she could get into heaven."

The nun called me a heretic and an apostate. From then on, she'd make the sign of the cross whenever she saw me and turn away her face. "Get away from me. I can't look at you. You have the Devil inside of you."

"Why? Because I said that Christ died for her sins so she could get into heaven? Why do you think Christ died, Sister Catherine?"

She arranged a private meeting with the chaplain, Father Murray, so he could "straighten me out." For starters, I told him I wouldn't call him "Father" but "Mister Murray," citing Matthew 23:9. A cordial, amiable, soft-spoken young gentleman, he wasn't at all the pedantic, harsh, or preachy type I'd expected. He listened as much as he spoke.

"What's your objection to the last rites for your mother?"

"If people needed sacraments such as the last rites to get into heaven, Christ wouldn't have left heaven to come and die on the cross. He could've stayed up there and let us get to him through sacraments, good deeds, sacrifices, prayers, masses, indulgences, and torment in purgatory."

"As long as we're not sure, we might as well pile on everything we've got."

"We *are* sure. Jesus said, 'I am the way, the truth, and the life. No man comes to the Father but by me. I am the door. By me if any man enter in, he shall be saved.' He never said 'by me and sacraments, masses, purgatory, etc.' He said, 'by me.'"

"The origin of purgatory is from the Book of Wisdom, which says, 'Pray for the dead that they may be delivered.'"

"That's an apocryphal book. It was written before Christ died on the cross and rose again to deliver the believers who had died awaiting the Messiah. Those were people like Abraham and the beggar at his bosom. But when Jesus died, he said, 'It is finished.'"

"Florence, we get the sacraments from Christ's appointment of Saint Peter as the first pope. He said, 'Go into the word and teach all nations, baptizing them, teaching them.'"

"Mr. Murray, the rest of that sentence is 'teaching them to observe all things, whatsoever I have taught you.' Christ never said, 'Make up your own rules.'"

I left him with the suggestion that he read his own Bible and pray to God himself about it.

I never heard from Mr. Murray again. Months later I read in the *Paterson Evening News* that he had resigned his position as chaplain and left the priesthood.

Chapter 25

TOTO'S APOLOGY

I WATCHED TELEVISION at home alone that Saturday evening. Mom remained in the hospital, and Pop had gone out to visit some buddies. Toto stopped by, asking for Pop. I didn't even offer him a chair. I simply tried to dismiss him with "Sorry, I'll tell him you were here."

Toto said, "Wait. I'm glad for this opportunity to talk to you in private. I've been feeling guilty about something that happened long ago, and I owe you an apology."

Afraid he might be referring to the rape, I became uncomfortable. I'd hoped he thought I'd forgotten what had occurred when I was so young. I'd rather forego the apology than have a confrontation about it now. But he went on. "When I baptized you, I promised your mother I'd give her fifty dollars a year toward your college education until you turned twenty-one. When you were a baby, fifty dollars was considered a tidy sum." Still in his winter overcoat, he sat down on the arm of an overstuffed chair. "I kept my promise until you graduated from high school, when your mom said you didn't want to go to college. Then I stopped buying the savings bonds I'd been giving her for you every birthday and Christmas."

I recalled the closing on the house when I was ten and the $500 down payment Mom had made by redeeming $25 savings bonds. Now I knew where those had come from. It also explained the beige envelopes she would stash into the china closet after he visited. As customary when minors were payees, the bonds had been issued so either Mom or I could redeem them.

If he had given Mom fifty dollars times seventeen years, by the time I graduated high school, she'd received about $850. This was more than twice the tuition money that would have put me through teachers' college. Although Toto assumed I knew of his generosity, nobody had ever told me. I suppose I should have thanked him then, but I stood there too baffled to remember my manners. This unrealized scholarship would be another secret I'd have to keep that involved my Sicilian godfather.

Next time I went to see Mom, she was awake. After I fed and groomed her, she said, "Do you remember the day you got home late from school, and nobody answered when I phoned the school? Tell me the truth. I can't do anything to you now. Where were you really?"

"I was in school, Mom."

After a long hesitation, she sighed, looked me in the face, and said, "I believe you."

Then Mom became comatose. Who would have imagined a year earlier that now we'd no longer be able to communicate? "I'm glad her older children moved far away and aren't here to see Mama like this," I told Pop.

True, she had never taken good care of her health. Since her hospitalization for the burst appendix two decades earlier, she had shunned medical checkups. Still, this once-vibrant woman had seemed indestructible. Rarely catching so much as a common cold, she hadn't taken a sick day from work in more than twenty years.

Yet she'd reached the point where families pray, "Dear God, please take her." The illness had swollen her face and neck, distorting them beyond recognition. This once gorgeous, youthful-looking, middle-aged woman had become a hideous, emaciated sixty-pound "vegetable." On my daily visits, powerless to reverse the malady, I could only sit by and watch her grow worse.

At home, I slept on our living room couch to be within twelve feet of the only phone we had. At 5:45 AM I awoke but lay there in the dark, bemoaning Mama's condition. Then I saw her reclined on another couch across the room. Surrounded by light, she was lying with her head to the right, her feet to the left. Her dress was unlike any I'd ever seen before. Blue-gray velvet with long sleeves, it had several wide layers of white-lace ruffles at the wrists and neckline. Pinned neatly in place, her wavy, black hair clung below both temples just above her high cheekbones. This was nothing like the loose, flowing hairstyle she'd always worn. Her huge, sparkling hazel eyes were wide open. For the first time in weeks, she looked right at me and smiled. Gone were the scars of her illness. Gone the swelling that had distorted her face and neck. Her weight back to normal, she looked strong and completely healed.

"Mama, you look wonderful."

"I'm all better now," she said in her native Italian. "Don't be sad for me anymore. I don't feel any pain, and I'm in a much better place."

Just then the telephone rang. Once again in a darkened room I felt my way over to answer on the first ring. The charge nurse at the hospital was calling. "Please have someone from the family come here right away," she said in a detached, businesslike voice. "I can't give you any information over the phone."

Mama had passed away at 5:30.

Pop met with Mr. Delatorre, the funeral director, alone. They made all the arrangements without conveying any details to me. Barely out of my teens, I had never been to a funeral home or seen a deceased person before.

Three days later, at the viewing in the mortuary, Mama's youngest half brother, Joe, stood next to me. "She's lying with her head to the right," he observed. "Usually people are laid out with their feet to the right. They have her laid out backwards."

Overhearing this, Mr. Delatorre walked over to us. "It was done that way to hide scars. We custom-made her dress with layers of white, extra-wide lace ruffles at the neckline for the same reason."

I looked closely at the blue-gray velvet dress and the hairdo the mortuary staff had chosen. These looked exactly as I had seen them in my vision the morning Mama passed away.

"Why is her hair pinned at the sides like that?" I asked.

"Oh, our hairdresser thought it looked neater."

I didn't tell this story to many people. I suspected most would dismiss it as an early-morning dream. Some might say I was imagining things, possibly hallucinating. Could a dream or even a hallucination have predicted Mama's exact dress, hairstyle, and unusual way of being laid out?

I don't know how to explain the vision. I've never claimed to have prophetic gifts of any kind. I have asked several trusted doctors of theology about this event. They assured me I wasn't mingling in the realm of a "familiar spirit." The vision, they surmised, was an isolated, special assurance from beyond that Mama truly was restored, happy, and in a much better place.

The Italian word for goodbye, *addio*, literally means "to God." How appropriate to say, "To God, Mama."

Chapter 24

AL

ON FRIDAYS AT the bank, the 6:00 to 8:00 PM time period proved busiest. Scores of customers who worked during the week came in to cash their paychecks.

One evening a family consisting of a fifty-year-old woman, two men in their forties, and a twenty-three-year-old male filed in. They spotted my name etched in a plastic desk plate at my workstation. Despite the long line of customers at my teller window, they waited their turn to see me.

"I can talk to you in Italian?" the woman said. She spoke the dialect of the city of Abruzzi, similar enough to Sicilian that I indicated I understood it well. She looked taller to me than most Italian women I'd known.

"Miss Calderone, this is my son, Bruno."

I greeted him and then waited on them with the usual customer courtesy. They soon left. Bruno, however, returned alone. "Missy, I can have change of a quarter? Need nickel for parking meter." His grin revealed a set of broken, ill-spaced teeth the color of coffee grounds. The blackheads that dotted his coarse, oily forehead made him look as though he'd been sprayed with miniature shrapnel. His rumpled rust-brown shirt hosted random drops of crusted mozzarella cheese and clam sauce like paint on an artist's palette.

"Here is your change, sir. Who is next, please?"

This family became regulars on Fridays at rush hour, each time waiting in line at my window, cashing checks, and leaving. Each time Bruno would return and ask for nickels to feed the parking meter. One Friday, as I completed their transactions, I handed his mother a quarter's worth of coins. "So that nobody has to wait in this long line again, here are some nickels for the parking meter."

They exchanged puzzled looks.

Four months after Mama's death, Pop still wouldn't allow me to play the radio or TV. He also banned playing a guitar or singing when Eddie Fitzmaurice and friends came by. "To mourn your mother properly, I expect you to dress completely in black for a year. We will go visit her grave together every Sunday afternoon."

One Sunday I arrived home from church to find Pop watching his favorite opera on the same TV he'd forbidden me to view.

"Well, Pop, I guess you realized that avoiding music or TV can't bring Mom back." I continued the cemetery visits but ceased the black mourning clothes. "In America, that custom doesn't prevail, Pop. Black clothes are depressing to my coworkers and everyone else around. And they won't bring Mom back either."

For three years, Eddie had often reminded me that his friend Al Kolee* said he'd like to ask me out. But Al could never find the courage. A member of my high school graduating class, Al was known for his calm, quiet shyness. Eddie planned group trips to events we all enjoyed, such as stock car races. He managed to make sure Al and I wound up sitting together at the stadium or in the car. One evening I sat next to Al in Eddie's convertible, and I shared my Christian faith with Eddie, the driver. In his good-natured way, Eddie reacted by laughing and addressing me as "Saint Florence."

"Listen to her, Ed," Al said. "She's telling you the truth."

God's Word prospers in the thing he sends it out to do. I then turned my attention to Al. The following Sunday he started driving me to my church services. Now Eddie had two close friends to bug him about his salvation.

Al had reached his twenty-second birthday, the age at which the U.S. government conscripted eligible men into military service. Within weeks, he received his draft notice and headed straight for my house with it.

"I want to get married before I go into the army. Then if I'm stationed far away, I can take you with me."

Since Toto's attack, I hadn't yet been completely able to dismiss my fear of marriage. Al's shyness helped ease my terror of male aggressiveness enough that I accepted his proposal. Still, I'd struggled with Mom's prediction that worthwhile men would only marry virgins and would consider me "trash."

Radiating happiness, Al started counting the days to the June wedding he planned for us. As it approached, so did my panic. Could I get past my phobia and become that chaste yet sizzling, ideal bedroom partner he'd hoped for? He had a right to the unvarnished truth and the option to change his mind. Without naming names, I told him about Toto's violent act and its enduring effects.

"You were four years old? What a monster he was!" Al hesitated a minute, to absorb the impact, then put his arm around me. "Don't worry, Babe, I'm fully committed to you, no matter what. God drew us to each other. God will make this work."

Was my mother's prediction wrong? "So it doesn't bother you if I'm not a virgin?"

"You're my sweet, wonderful girl—everything I've ever wanted—and I love you."

That had gone a lot easier than I'd ever imagined. But when I informed the Nobleman of my wedding plans, his reaction shocked me. He waved clenched fists and shouted expletives. "What gets into your head? Where do this man's people come from?"

"One grandfather came from Switzerland and the other from Alsace-Lorraine."

"No. I want you to marry a nice Italian boy. I have one picked out for you. The wedding is all planned."

"None of my siblings married Italians. You didn't object then. Who's this man you say you've picked out?"

"You know him and his parents. He's a guy from Abruzzi who works with me at the dye house. You see them in the bank every Friday night."

"Oh, my gosh, you mean Bruno, the kid with the horrible complexion and pointy, dark-brown teeth?"

"If you won't marry him, I'll boycott your wedding. Then in case of death or divorce, you no longer have a father."

I'd often told Pop nobody goes up to God before birth and asks to be Sicilian or Swiss or French. We take whatever nationality God gives us.

"Pop, I don't even like Bruno."

"You don't have to like him. Your father has to like him for you."

"My father doesn't have to sit across from him at the breakfast table every morning, nor have his babies. Pop, he turns my stomach."

"You're making me lose face with his relatives. I already promised him and his mother you'd marry him. I have to see this guy at work every day. You don't know how stubborn your father can be."

I thought of my mother's thirty-seven-year-long marriage to Pop and my grandmother's briefer one to Ventura. Each felt enslaved by men they wouldn't have chosen. I found it touching yet almost insulting that Pop thought he had to find a husband for me. As much as he'd meant well, I couldn't let myself go along with his plan.

Our tug-of-war escalated into the only major confrontation I'd ever have with Pop. While I was at it, I asked his version of something Mama had accused him of for years. "Pop, you've never acknowledged having a second sister. Was Mom right about that? Is it true that you and your older sister, Paola, killed her?"

"Giovanna wasn't supposed to die. The woman who did it messed everything up."

"Who was that?"

"Annina, the midwife. She botched up the abortion, and my little sister hemorrhaged. The nearest hospital was a hundred miles away. Giovanna would've bled to death anyway. Paola brought me my revolver." He looked down, and his voice dropped to a mumble. "I had to finish it off."

"It was a mercy killing?"

"It was restoring our family's good name."

I recalled having met midwife Annina who'd moved downstairs from Grace and Joe Lobo. "Pop, was that why Mom got so nervous when she saw Annina in Paterson?"

"No. Your mother had hired her to get rid of you before you were born. I got home and stopped everything just in time."

"Thanks, Pop. So Mom's major reason for evading the Lobo family for ten years was to avoid Annina."

"Yes. Annina also delivered my son Gerlando, who died after eighteen months in Palermo's hospital."

Gerlando, the first—the baby Mom told me had perished in her arms at six months. More reason for Mom to duck contact with Annina. The midwife would know that child's real birth date, but she apparently never took him in to register his birth. Those secrets remain buried with her. I spared Pop the information that Mom's details regarding this infant didn't match what he was telling me now.

As for Pop's faith system, he regarded church attendance as his weekly social outing. He put most of his trust in horoscopes and good luck charms, such as horseshoes and goldfish. His only mention of God was in maledictions.

"Pop, what do you believe happens to us when we die?"

"Once we're dead, all things are forgiven."

"You don't believe that unrepentant killers will be punished?"

"No. I've been in sulfur mines more than a hundred feet underground and never saw the Devil. So there can't be a hell."

This reasoning came from the brain-damaged man who'd scold me for putting ice cubes in the sink. He thought ice chips would clog the drain.

Now our family history was repeating itself, pitting yet another headstrong daughter at odds with parental authority about a wedding. I considered eloping, but I knew how heart shattering that would be for Pop. Also, because Al was an only child, his wedding would have to be memorable for his parents.

"I inherited your stubbornness, Pop," I said. "My wedding to Al is June 8, 1958, at Calvary Baptist Church in Clifton. If you're not there, nobody's going to ask, 'Where's the bride?' They'll ask, 'Where's the bride's father?'"

At the church where I'd attended the revival meeting three years earlier, I was married in a pure white lace dress. Pop walked me up the aisle and enjoyed the role of host at the modest reception afterward. It was geographically and economically inconvenient for any of my siblings to attend.

Having distanced themselves from me for abandoning their religion, most of my other relatives and school chums stayed away. But Eddie Fitzmaurice, Al's closest buddy, brought friends to sit on the bride's side of the church for me.

The Nobleman was the only person present who was related to me.

The Nobleman and his daughter leave for her wedding.

The Nobleman and Florence leaving for her wedding

Above: Eddie Fitzmaurice and friends after the reception. Eddie is front row extreme right. Back row in dark jacket is Jim Van Wyk, another childhood friend.

Chapter 25

MY FIRST MARRIAGE

UPON RETURNING FROM our honeymoon, Al packed for his twelve weeks in army boot camp. Three months later, he was transferred to Fort Bliss, Texas. I left my job at First Federal to follow him.

In El Paso, I found work at a bank and soon became steeped in the bilingual culture of the Mexican border. I studied and practiced Spanish every day, and Al bought me a Spanish Bible.

Almost two years later, we had our precious daughter, Joleen, as Al prepared to return to civilian life back in Paterson.

He lamented that he'd never realized any of his career dreams from childhood. He'd wanted to be a corporate lawyer but couldn't because he'd flunked Latin in high school.

"Al, your high school yearbook says 'future engineer.' What happened to that?"

"I scored too low on the math portion of the entrance exam at Newark College of Engineering."

"What was your third choice?"

"To repair jet airplanes."

I convinced him to enroll in Teterboro School of Aeronautics for his associate's degree. I'd work part-time in a bank's bookkeeping department while his mom watched the kids. Upon graduation, he found work as an aircraft mechanic with Pan Am World Airways. By then, we had our son, Al III, and we got to do some inexpensive traveling.

We saw parts of England, Germany, France, Switzerland, Italy, Bermuda, Canada, Mexico, and Hawaii. We also visited most states in North America. Not bad for a slum kid who'd never traveled more than a mile from home during childhood.

An influx of Latin American families arrived in our Paterson area neighborhood. Now a stay-at-home mom, I was usually the only English-speaking person on our block by day. I continued studying Spanish out of library books and was exposed to it in conversations with neighbors. I read my Spanish and Italian Bibles from cover to cover. These would come in handy years later when I volunteered for the Billy Graham Crusade's foreign language section.

Eventually, as street drugs became more prevalent, our neighborhood saw a steep rise in the violent crime rate. The scene of a heinous robbery and multiple murders that were unjustly blamed on boxer Rubin Hurricane Carter happened just three blocks from our home. Closer yet, a corner grocer's son was shot dead in a local mid-afternoon holdup. Our downstairs neighbor, a next-door neighbor, and a cousin on our street suffered muggings in daylight hours. To escape the danger and live closer to Al's job at Kennedy Airport, we moved to Long Island.

At age thirty-seven, Al was diagnosed with premature hardening of the arteries. Apparently, it ran in his family, along with a love for rich, fattening foods. Doctors warned that unless he lost weight, he wouldn't live five more years. Al continued to ignore his doctor's advice and to gain more weight. Bracing for the possibility that I'd have to support a family without him, I took civil service exams and started working at the county social services department. Al III, our younger child, was now fourteen.

One fringe benefit my job offered was a 75 percent tuition reimbursement for work-related college courses. Although in total denial about his health problems, Al remained supportive of my quest for a degree. I took course work in ten-week seminars that lasted all day each Saturday. I also managed to challenge some courses by passing comprehensive college-level exams. In night school, I took two semesters of college Spanish so I could read and write it. I received a bachelor of science degree in business administration with minors in social sciences and humanities from the University of New York at Albany.

Then I took child protective certificate courses from Cornell in Ithaca and numerous continuing education credits in creative writing. I had yet to experience teaching. By this time Long Island had a glut of unemployed teachers.

On a pleasant Saturday evening, we got a surprise phone call from Eddie Fitzmaurice. "Flo, I wanted you to be the first to know; I'm a born-again Christian."

"Eddie, how did it happen?"

"I got to thinking about what you said years ago, when Al said, 'Listen to her, Ed; she's telling you the truth.' I started reading the Bible and going to church, and now I know I'm saved."

It had taken about twenty-one years for those seeds to bear fruit. It always amazes me to see God's faithfulness in action when he gives the increase to the seed that was planted.

Al had helped me complete my degree and showed us many beautiful world capitals. On May 1, 1980, he suffered a massive heart attack right in front of me. I learned the emergency meaning of the word "*Mayday!*" as the rescue squad spent forty-five frantic minutes trying to revive him. At age forty-four, he was pronounced dead on arrival at the hospital.

Few people attended Al's wake or funeral. The one friend who made the eighty-mile drive from New Jersey to offer condolences was Eddie Fitzmaurice. It took me at least three months to get over the denial stage of my grieving process. I knew Al had died; I'd watched his casket being lowered into the ground. I just couldn't accept that it wasn't all a nightmare from which I'd awaken to resume my normal life.

The following month our son's high school graduation took place, and I sat in the stands alone. Then both children attended local colleges as I faced our house mortgage payments. Through rough, lean times, God never let us down.

The kids started socializing with their friends, leaving me home alone evenings and weekends. "Will you be okay, Mom?"

"Of course. I'm not a baby. Don't worry about me."

Caring coworkers tried to get me to go out with them to nightclubs, but I wasn't interested. Friends from church invited us to dinner on rare occasions, such as Thanksgiving. Otherwise, they mostly kept to themselves and their immediate families.

One day I checked local classified ads for unmarried Christian support groups where I might meet people in my situation. I phoned the first one, listed as "North Shore Christian Singles." A man describing himself as a fifty-year-old pastor answered.

"I'm calling about the Christian singles group," I said.

"Oh, is that still in the paper? My ex-wife started that. Then she left me. Now I'm all alone and so lonely."

"So the group has disbanded?"

"Yes, but do you like cabin cruisers? I'd love to have you join me on mine some time. You sound cute."

Why did I doubt that this man really was a pastor and that there really was an ex-wife and that he really was lonely? There goes that bitter, skeptic nature of mine. I declined his gracious invitation.

By phone, I answered another ad aimed at Christian singles of all ages. "Would a forty-four-year-old fit in with your group?"

"Oh yes. That's exactly the same age as most of our members."

When I arrived, I found a meeting room occupied entirely by nice folks whose grandchildren were older than I was.

The next ad I read was for what claimed to be a Spirit-filled Christian prayer group. "You might be unmarried due to demon possession," their leader said. "We hold biweekly tent meetings to cast out demons and drive them into the swine. Come, join us, sister. Bring your own pig. You'll be richly blessed."

I didn't have a pig; didn't join them; didn't get that rich blessing.

Part 5

MORE MIRACLES

Chapter 26

THE KISS I LEAST EXPECTED

IT SEEMED COMPLICATED. I knew I was hooked, but then so was every female between ages twenty and fifty in our Long Island government agency. We admired Terry's intelligence and courageous independence. Ruggedly handsome in his early forties, this ex-navy chief was a single, custodial parent. His staunch opposition to dating subordinates and coworkers kept him beyond reach.

Now a widow and eighteen months older than Terry, I had acquired a horrible reputation—that of a whistle-blower. When I turned down overtures from Ray,* a married executive, the honcho retaliated by exiling me to the worst possible work site. Tripling my commuting distance, this outlying branch office sat upstairs from the county morgue. My complaint to the union sparked warnings from upper management to all male bosses: "Avoid even the appearance of friendship with blabbermouth Flo."

Unaware of the mandate and with two strikes against me, I reported to my new department, which Terry supervised. The wind churned swirls of dust in the vast parking area near the structure's entryway. Upon my arrival, the pungent smell of formaldehyde permeated the building and irritated my nostrils. To my cordial "Good morning, Mr. Blake," Terry replied, "Comb your hair. You look like something the cat dragged in."

When I asked work-related questions, he quipped, "I'd love to help you out, Flo. Which way did you come in?"

One afternoon several months later, a firefighter approached my desk. "You have to leave immediately, ma'am; this building's on fire."

Upon reaching the crowded parking lot, I asked some coworkers, "Did Terry Blake make it out OK?"

The guys laughed and then one replied, "The first thing Terry asked when he got here was, 'Did Florence get out OK?'"

Hmmm. Five hundred other people worked there, yet this grouch who was polite to everybody else thought of me?

By that summer, my reputation for rebuffing Ray's advances intrigued coworker Carl,* who regarded it a challenge. Since I outranked him, he wasn't concerned about being accused of sexual harassment. He'd press for dates, I'd decline. He'd back off for two weeks and then start the pressure again. One day I asked God how to deal with the Carl problem. I didn't want to file another union grievance. Office Casanovas rarely misbehave around witnesses, and I'd hate to harm Carl's livelihood.

The still, small voice said, "Terry Blake."

Terry Blake? I couldn't have gotten that right. The guy with the ex-sailor's vocabulary and the tattoos? Sure, I'm madly in love with him, but isn't he the one who hates me?

The message seemed unmistakable. "Terry Blake."

At the close of this particular workday, I confided to Terry my exasperation with Carl.

"There's a simple solution, Flo. Tell him you're dating someone else."

"But I'm not really, Terry. Am I?"

He put his arm around my shoulder. "Yes, you are, Flo." Then Terry admitted that even before we'd ever met, he'd received instructions from our former commissioner to avoid me. Terry's disdain for Lothario Ray had labeled me heroic for rejecting a high-ranking egomaniac.

In the almost-deserted parking lot, Terry walked me to my car. "What would you do if I grabbed you and kissed you right now, Flo?"

"I'd kiss you back."

Wow! God does work in mysterious ways.

Eight weeks later, despite the unofficial order placing me off-limits, Terry and I were married. Many younger, prettier coworkers were stunned that he'd picked me rather than one of them. "That marriage can't possibly last six months," they said. But were they wrong! Our awesome God blessed us with more than twenty-seven happy years together. Maybe at first it seemed complicated, but nothing's too complicated for God, who can make our most impossible dreams come true.

Terry Blake at a Western-themed office party

Decades before, when the navy transferred him from Bremerton, Washington to San Diego, California, Terry had fallen in love with Oregon. When traveling through southern Oregon, he'd stopped for lunch and thought its lush mountains belonged in storybooks. "If I ever buy acreage, it will be in southern Oregon."

Reality has a way of overtaking our wishes, and by 1981 we still lived and worked on Long Island. We visited Oregon on every vacation in the early to late 1980s. On one trip, he bought me a cherished souvenir, a mandolin and an instruction booklet. Not having had many toys as a child, I regard musical instruments as a respectable excuse to play with grown-up toys. I had picked up some basic skills on Mil's guitar and found it easy to adapt to another stringed instrument. I can see why Mom liked mandolin music. It's Mediterranean but also bluegrass. Today I use it to write and accompany songs God gives me to his glory.

Since Terry so longed to live in Oregon, we relocated when the time was right. Our children, now grown, preferred to stay back East where all their friends were.

Terry built our house in Oregon, and God surrounded him with believers. The electrician who wired the house, the man who poured the concrete foundation, the gravel deliveryman, and local merchants all invited him to church. He was baptized on September 11, 1988, in the Rogue River. For the past ten years Terry served as a deacon in our congregation.

But when we were still new to Oregon, I took civil service tests in English and Spanish. God gave me employment with state social service agencies.

In the summer of 1989, my oldest brother, Ang, who lived in Southern California, wrote me a letter. Now a private pilot, he planned to rent a small plane and fly to see us on his next vacation. He had set it for early September. The week before his scheduled visit, a wind shear knocked his tiny aircraft out of the skies and crashed it to the airport runway. Both he and his passenger died of multiple burns.

In another part of the world, the Nobleman never received news of his eldest son's death. My other siblings felt there was no point in upsetting Pop. He'd feel obligated to attend the funeral and wasn't up to traveling long distances.

The Nobleman's second wedding in Casteltermini

Chapter 27

HOW WE BECAME MILLIONAIRES

POP, THE NOBLEMAN, had realized his fondest dreams. He'd finally returned home. Once again, he strolled down familiar streets of his native city. In the center of Casteltermini stood the flour mill founded by his father and the spaghetti factory emblazoned with the name "Calderone and Company" in Italian. The family sulfur mine he had once managed still exported massive supplies of that mineral. But Pop no longer owned any interests in these enterprises. His rights to them had been wrested from him by the Fascists. Nor did he still own the palatial villa with servants and his beloved horses. These too had been stripped from him by Fascism in 1931, when Don Angelo offered his sons choices that Pop had rejected.

Still, upon his repatriation, he found that his surname commanded respectful bows and "Good morning, Cavaliere Calderone" from local gentry in the marketplace.

His return occurred in 1960, two years after Mom's death. The Nobleman had flown to Sicily to remarry. His new bride, age fifty-eight and never previously married, preferred to reside there. He lived on the proceeds from the sale of his house in Paterson, plus three pensions. These were from Social Security, the American Textile Workers Union, and the knighthood once bestowed upon him by King Victor Emanuel III.

We wrote back and forth for several years. For a while Pop thought I had stopped writing, since my letters weren't getting past the Rome post office and through to Casteltermini. Certain postal employees abroad believed letters from Americans might contain cash. Nobody knew how many letters were waylaid. I tried a fiendish gimmick. Italians harbor a deep respect for death, and its well-known symbol of mourning was a black border around an envelope. When I started drawing black borders around the envelopes I mailed to Pop, they reached him. The sight of the black edging didn't upset Pop. He assumed I'd remained in bereavement for my deceased spouse, Al.

I found Pop's letters unintentionally amusing. He'd say things like "From my window I can see the church where each year we crucify the risen Christ and our local Police Department." "Yesterday I painted my apartment along with my wife, my brother-in-law, and my nephews."

Then he'd say he had nothing more to add but would continue writing for four more pages. He'd sign off with "Your most affectionate Papa, Giovanni C. Believe me always."

Eventually, his letters began showing confusion. "Give my regards to your husband, Bob, [that's my sister's husband's name], and your three children, [I never had more than two]." He'd assign them names of various siblings' children. He'd inquire about the health status of people who had died decades earlier, some before I was born. I still wrote to him, but each letter he sent back contained heartbreak.

Valentine's Day of 1991 brought us sad news. At age ninety-six, the Nobleman had died. Operation Desert Storm, (the first Gulf War) raged, and U.S. activation of military airbases in the Mediterranean placed Sicily off limits. Deemed too close to "no fly" zones, all nonmilitary flights to Palermo Airport were temporarily discontinued. Compounding our grief, we learned that none of his children in America could attend his funeral.

In the process I learned another hard lesson. Even beyond the airport closure drawback, another obstacle I hadn't considered would have prevented my attending. My passport had remained unused since the days my first husband, Al, worked for Pan Am. It had expired, and even an expedited process would have required several more days to reinstate it. I could find no exceptions—not even a death in the family—to bypass the passport's expiration status. I now advise anyone who has loved ones abroad to keep passports updated in case of unexpected contingencies.

A year later I received a phone call at work from my spouse, Terry. "We have an official-looking letter from Sicily. It's typed in Italian, but I recognize names and numbers. It lists your Pop's five children and the figure '12 million' next to each name."

That night my sister, Lee, phoned from Cape Cod. "They've managed to place our inheritance completely out of our reach." The official letters imposed seemingly insurmountable restrictions and deadlines heirs had to meet to claim inheritances. We each had to furnish a *certificato familiare* along with duly notarized affidavits of authenticity typed in both Italian and English. Within thirty days of the date on their letter, these documents had to be received at Casteltermini's municipal courthouse. Missing this deadline meant forfeiting the entire sixty-million to them.

"Even airmail takes at least a week to travel one way from Sicily to us, Lee. That leaves a two-week window to meet the requirements."

We knew the words *certificato familiare* meant "familial certificate." But what was it? How and where would we get them, especially on such short notice?

"Yeah, Flo, and they know we'll probably never unearth a notary public who just happens to type in both English and Italian."

But the hand of God was in this. "Lee, you're talking to an Oregon notary who can type in both languages. I'll call the Italian Consulate Office in San Francisco and ask about those familial certificates."

Next morning, I phoned them. When I recounted our plight, a gentleman with a charming continental accent chuckled.

"Someone puts obstacles in your way so they can keep your money. In America, a *certificato familiare* is nothing more than a birth certificate. Get copies of all birth certificates of your father's children. If they bear the names of both parents, you have your familial certificates."

By priority mail, Lee sent me our birth records. Ah, the beauty of the Italian language! It doesn't have any peculiar points, such as inverted question marks or tildes as Spanish does. It's also purely phonetic. I could type practically anything in Italian using the same typewriter I'd use for English.

Not legally permitted to notarize my own signature, I typed the bilingual statements and asked a colleague to notarize them. For my siblings, I typed the affidavits, notarized them, and shipped copies to Casteltermini's municipal courthouse.

Within a few weeks, we all became millionaires. We received our checks from a bank in Casteltermini for 12 million. I should clarify that this was 12 million lire, which in American money came to about $1,800 each. Ang's kids split his share three ways.

Terry and I blew ours on car repairs.

Chapter 28

ONE TURBULENT HOLIDAY

IT SCARED ME. I'd never heard Terry say that before. During all our years of marriage, he'd seemed impervious to illness. He'd shake a cold in two days. That particular Sunday afternoon, however, coughing occasionally, he took an extra-long nap on the couch. At first, I left him alone to rest. But when I reentered the room, Terry muttered, "Florence, I'm sick."

I touched his forehead. "It feels too warm. I'm phoning Dr. Robertson's office."

The answering service suggested going to the emergency room, so I drove Terry to Providence ER. A staff physician examined him, diagnosed pneumonia, and prescribed an antibiotic. He sent Terry home with "If you haven't improved by Tuesday, call Dr. Robertson."

Midday on Tuesday, Terry phoned me at work. He had seen Dr. Robertson, who had done x-rays and was admitting him to Providence Hospital. He needed me to drive him there, where he'd see lung specialist Dr. Blackmon. It was two days before Christmas 1997 during a cold snap in southern Oregon. Before leaving work, I phoned our church office. "Terry Blake is at Providence with pneumonia. Please pray."

After he examined Terry, Dr. Blackmon seemed confident. "You have some excess fluid in your lungs. We'll drain that, and you should be much better by morning. I can't guarantee you'll be home for Christmas, but let's hope so."

I kissed Terry good night and headed home to feed steers, chickens, and pets on our small ranch.

The next morning before work I visited my husband. He was not "much better" as predicted. He looked worse. Convincing myself that these things took time, I headed to my job. But when I returned later, I didn't like what I saw or heard from Dr. Blackmon.

"I'm sorry, Mrs. Blake, but this is one tough strain of pneumonia. We drain one liter from his lungs, and they fill up with two more. We'll drain them again and strengthen his medication. This may take hours."

God provided neighbors to feed our animals that evening. This allowed me to stay with Terry until after 10:30 PM. Dr. Blackmon remained after I left. This case had become such a challenge that his quest for a cure took over.

On December 25, the same kind neighbors who had fed the animals for us phoned me in Terry's room.

"Flo, if you'd like to have Christmas dinner with us and our family, feel free to stop in. We hate to see you spendin' the holiday eatin' by yourself. We got plenty of food here."

"Thanks so much, but I'll be fine. I just don't want to be too far away from Terry right now."

The doctor asked me to wait elsewhere while he and a technician performed another procedure. I sat alone, listening to "White Christmas" and "Jingle Bells" on the intercom, and munched a hot turkey sandwich in an almost-empty cafeteria. Upstairs at Terry's bedside, monitoring their progress on an ultrasound screen, they drained still more lung fluid. By next morning, it had all returned.

For several days, Terry remained hospitalized and grew worse. Dr. Blackmon was stumped. All his state-of-the-art medical treatments refused to conquer this invincible germ. Prayer chains kept busy. Our pastor stopped by and prayed. Terry's buddy Rich visited daily and walked with him down hospital corridors. Rich knew it wasn't advisable for pneumonia patients to stay too still for long periods.

Several days after his hospital admission, I found my usually cheerful husband lying silent, his face turned away, ignoring my arrival. Rich phoned me at home late that evening. "What happened? Terry wouldn't get out of bed today, wouldn't walk, and wouldn't talk to me. It's like he doesn't want to fight this anymore."

"I noticed the same thing, Rich. He seems to have given up. Please keep praying hard."

I hung up the phone and said the tearful oration: "Dear God, nothing's too hard for you. Please reverse this horrible condition. Please cure Terry."

I'm surprised at the immediacy with which that still, small voice responds. "Florence, clean the humidifier."

By now, I should've known better, but I still wasn't good at recognizing the still, small voice. Furthest from my mind was some silly plastic appliance set in a dim corner of the floor. Where had this thought come from? God knew Terry's condition. He knew I wiped the humidifier with soapy dishcloths whenever I refilled it. Convinced the message couldn't be from God, I brushed it aside and continued praying.

But in his awesome kindness, the Holy Spirit wouldn't let this humidifier issue go away. I walked over to what looked like a sparkling-clean styrene appliance. I unplugged it, wheeled it over to the sink, took it apart, and scrubbed each piece. Then I aimed a light into the lowest section beneath the water chambers, where overflows spilled. There, floating in an inch of water, was a collection of white, moldy substance I'd never seen before. Our humidifier had been blowing tainted moisture into the air Terry inhaled while he took mid-afternoon naps.

Old newscasts flashed into my mind. Legionnaires' disease, a lethal strain of pneumonia, had originally derived from unsanitary cooling ducts that infected a convention center. Could this be happening in our house?

Next morning, I rushed to find Dr. Blackmon as he completed paperwork at the nurse's station. "Doctor, I'm not medically knowledgeable, so please forgive my ignorance. But might Terry have Legionnaires' disease?"

"No, we ruled out Legionnaires'. He hasn't been in a hotel recently where the system's ductwork might be contaminated."

"What if I told you I found an inch of moldy goop floating on the bottom of a humidifier twenty feet from where he naps?"

His eyes grew wider. "Take Mr. Blake off that IV," he told the nurse as he scribbled new directives. "Then get a sputum culture to the lab and start him on these oral meds. Tell them we're checking and treating for Legionella bacteria."

On New Year's Eve, the ninth day of Terry's hospital confinement, I found him grinning, on his feet, fully dressed. "Hey, Gorgeous, they're throwing me out of here. Whatever they did, it worked. Let's go home."

Terry's lab tests confirmed that he had indeed contracted Legionnaires' disease. Doctor Blackmon told me its survival rate was under 20 percent. But our God can do even the impossible. He gave us an extraordinary present that December.

"I put to death and I bring to life, I have wounded and I will heal, and no one can deliver out of my hand" (Deut. 32:39b NIV).

I thought of this one morning more than a decade after Terry's bout with Legionnaires' disease. Together we had witnessed the arrival of eleven more New Years. He had taken meticulous care to avoid respiratory illnesses. First in line at annual flu-shot clinics, he'd also made sure he'd kept up to date with vaccinations to prevent recurrence of pneumonia.

I also recalled that throughout her life my mother had harbored a Sicilian superstition I considered absurd. Like her friend Grace Lobo she attached hidden messages to dreams. Mom claimed this combination never failed. Whenever she dreamed about flowers, she would receive word that someone close to her had died.

Late in January of 2009, Terry contracted a severe bacterial infection that hospitalized him three times over a span of sixteen days. The morning of February 10, 2009, I awoke from a vivid dream. In it, I'd admired a sprawling array of multicolored flowers that swayed under rhythmic breezes. I had glanced down at the blossoms and had viewed Terry's face among them.

I'm so glad I'm not superstitious like Mom, I reminded myself. *Otherwise, I'd be worried that this dream meant bad news.* Hours later, I would repeat that to the hospital social worker at Terry's bedside. She said the virulent infection had damaged his heart, lungs, liver, kidneys, and brain.

ONE TURBULENT HOLIDAY

At 3:00 PM that Tuesday, I stared in disbelief. At age seventy-one, my beloved Terry abruptly departed this earth. I miss him, but I'm so grateful for the twenty-seven-plus years God granted me with him.

Chapter 29

WHAT'S NEXT?

DID I EVER get to teach school? Yes, in a community college. God is able to give us abundantly above all we ever ask or think (Eph. 3:20).

Thanks to the Internet, I've reconnected with some dear friends from childhood. Jim Van Wyk, Eddie Fitzmaurice's former neighbor, tells me Eddie passed away a few years ago. After I'd relocated to Oregon, Eddie had spent the last few years of his life trying to locate me. A few cast members from high school plays still e-mail me and phone me from the East Coast. Mrs. Bulmer's son, Bob, and now also his daughter remain heavily involved in the work of Christ's harvest.

People still ask whether I ever forgave my abusers. Looking back, I can see Mom had an all-too-brief, joyless life. None of us would have wanted to experience the circumstances she or her brothers endured early in their days.

Any fair-minded referee would say I was right because I "hungered and thirsted after righteousness." The physical bruises and the broken bones healed. The financial deceptions seem insignificant now.

As kids, my brothers had no idea how much harm they were causing. They grew up to be far better people as adults. Also, they've raised some outstanding children of their own. Jerry and Mil remember to e-mail me a happy birthday each year. Thanks to my awesome God, I got over Toto's brutal attack.

What was the hardest abuse to overcome? Probably Mom's prediction. "Nobody who gets to know you will ever like you. When people find out what you are really like, they will always hate you."

She must have been wrong. God blessed me with two husbands who were the best friends I ever had on earth. After decades of living with me, they not only loved me, but also liked me.

To the experts who say, "An abused child is bound to abuse her own children," I say, "Not necessarily. You'd know if you met my two wonderful, loving children and my precious stepchildren." The cycle of violence doesn't have to continue. If anything, the battered person can gain more empathy for the browbeaten.

Have I forgotten? Although for many years I tried to, the reminders kept returning. If I buried negative feelings, someone else kept digging them up. Enough Bible study and sound pastoral counseling have convinced me that we can handle reality better if we don't try to bury it, but admit that it happened and get past it.

Have I forgiven? I see that as a requirement. God paid attention to what humans would say and do in those regards. I remember Christ's admonition that the one without sin should cast the first stone. And because no one condemned the sinner after that, neither did he. If Stephen could say in Acts 7:50 (KJV) regarding those who stoned him to death, "Lord, lay not this sin to their charge," can I do less?

The abuses I survived on earth brought me closer to God, who delivered me and provided for me. He gave me ample evidence of his loving omnipresence. I think the best part of my existence is that I stand as a living argument against abortion. To those who say, "Why bring a child into a world where he's not wanted? Who needs poverty, rejection, or suffering?" I reply, "Praise God, despite experiencing abject poverty, scorn, rejection, and bigotry, I've had a wonderful sojourn here. And someday in heaven, I expect to see a saint I call Mama."

The End

LaVergne, TN USA
07 June 2010
185272LV00006B/2/P